THE NATURE OF HUMAN SOCIETY

THE MIND OF AFRICA

THE MIND OF AFRICA

W. E. Abraham

THE UNIVERSITY OF CHICAGO PRESS

The University of Chicago Press, Chicago 37
The University of Toronto Press, Toronto 5, Canada
Weidenfeld and Nicolson, London W.1, England

Printed in Great Britain

Dedicated
to us, the African people

CONTENTS

PREFACE

THE IDEA OF WRITING a book on the historic processes now moulding the continent of Africa grew upon me from several discussions and talks. The need to understand these processes is an insistent one. But to understand them one must analyse, and to analyse one must have a framework of leading ideas. Such a framework will help to reveal not only the titanic forces fulgurating in the continent but also those silent adjustments which together fix the countenance of a people, their principles, their attitudes, their desires and aversions, and their spring of action.

To analyse objectively, one needs to approximate to the externality of an outsider and the sensibility of one with an inward knowledge of things. I am an African, with responsive throbbings in the collective consciousness of Africa. But in being elected to a Fellowship at All Souls, I was able to appreciate that freedom, that consecution and relevance of thought, which physical insulation from the processes that one analyses helps.

I have not merely tried to describe, isolate, the forces at work in Africa, and to describe the people among whom the forces are unleashed. I have sought the fundamental framework within which these forces are set, that framework which reveals the people of Africa in their human condition in society. Every society has an ideology. It is the ideology of a society which yields those principles in the light of which significant events are judged to be significant. The first part of Chapter 1 explains and illustrates this function. This part of the book will inevitably appear a little abstract, but it is crucial, for it is what in a way holds the whole book together. In the second chapter I disentangle the theoretical complex underlying one African society and illustrate how and in what sense this theoretical complex is typical of Africa. In the third chapter the loss of independence and its regaining are studied in the light of the problems which they pose for Africa, and Africa's developing methods of coping with them. In the fourth and final chapter, certain problems of Africa are examined continent-wise, and African unity emerges as the setting which promises optimum solution.

To all those, both African and non-African, who in discussions have forced me to think about those currents which one feels, my deepest gratitude is due.

Above all, I am deeply grateful to Osagyefo Dr Kwame Nkrumah, who bestowed on this book the honour of reading it in typescript form.

Legon 1962   Willie E. Abraham

CHAPTER I

IDEOLOGY AND SOCIETY

Culture and the significance of events: The nature of culture—Historical considerations, humanism and rationality—Humanism and evolution—Essentialist and scientific analyses of man: Relations to politics—The foundation of society—The uses of culture: The African contact with Europe—The African contact with the Middle East—The traditional nature of Africa—Blue-print for paradise—Alleged pedigree.

ALL EVENTS OF LARGE significance take place within the setting of some culture, and indeed derive their significance from the culture in which they find themselves. It could therefore happen, and does indeed happen, that the same event, occurring as it were between the frontiers of two different cultures, should be invested with differing significance, with different capacities for arousing strong reaction, and with different capacities for determining the direction of policies arising therefrom. This immediately raises problems for a number of disciplines including, above all, history and social anthropology. The writing of the history of one culture from the milieu of another culture, which is not—relevant to the events and situations concerned—isomorphic, raises serious questions of cultural bias and distortion. It does not necessarily offer objectivity, and indeed could not offer it in any sense in which this involved freedom from cultural colour. In terms of objectivity, where it touches evaluation of facts and events, a cultural alien can only offer an alternative set of prejudices.

In periods of political transition, quick decisions and adaptation, in which African countries already find themselves, changes are strenuous, and many events are liable to appear bizarre. Their underlying rationales (for culture implies a rationale), and those silent adjustments which decide what are preserved and what are discarded, can only be brought to the surface by a clear exposition of the theoretical complex which sustains the culture involved. There is always such a complex, and it evinces itself in the interplay of cultural values and cultural discrimination; but of course, participation in the theory, as distinct from the practice, of the culture is made their preoccupation by only a minority of the people.

In Africa, there is a wealth of traditional general ideas, which make themselves felt both in the present-day theories of politics and society in that continent, and also, to the extent of independent countries at least, in their practice. It is important to carry out investigations into the theories of these cultures, and indeed it is such investigations which would reveal what portions of the West and the East, or indeed any foreign cultures, are likely to survive in Africa, and the pattern of the modifications which they are likely to suffer. Father Placide Tempels has pointed to this kind of study for the Balubas of the Congo.

I have not here attempted anything of the sort, but have rather, regarding this, tried to make out the importance of such investigations. In the process, it has not always been possible to avoid pointing out certain errors, some of them gross, into which a dull sense of the importance of such investigations has led. In a way, this is a theoretical work but hardly exclusively so. It is theoretical in so far as it enables one to see some of the questions which are raised, in a general way, for Africa. It also attempts to disentangle some of the complications resulting from the African contact with Europe and the Middle East, and deals with the prospects of the future based on the resultant complex. The future of Africa, if contemplated realistically, must be related to this complex, above all through its analysis. This way, some of the powerful purposes operating in Africa today can be studied, and the principles underlying them understood.

The word 'culture' is variously used. At its most inclusive, it is used to cover every possible aspect, public and private, of the life of a people. Used in this way, the term includes the whole of knowledge, the arts, science, technology, religions, morality, ritual, politics, literature, even etiquette and fashions, and such things as whether people clean their teeth three times a day or once. Even when the word is used in this way, it is not purely descriptive. When you hear it said that a cultured man gives his seat to a lady, you can be sure that you have heard, not a mere description, but a recommendation. Hence even in this broad usage, the word is used only in part to cover a description. In part, it is used to name an ideal or a cluster of ideals. Culture in this sense is inevitably divided into a public culture and a private culture. Public culture is the more rigorous, because it lays down an overt requirement for reasonable conformity. This demand is contained in the Akan (Ghanaian) sentences: *obi apow* and *obi mmpowee koraa*. To say *obii mmpowee koraa*, that he is uncultured, possibly boorish, is not simply to describe the sort of person, but almost in fact to accuse him. It is the same everywhere. It is correct to intend a reproof of someone in saying that he is uncultured.

There is, however, also a narrower use of the word, according to which culture is limited to what are called things of the mind. In this use, culture includes a mastery of literature, history, music, painting and sculpture. But this catalogue does not exhaust the content of culture. It is also required that the mind of the man who has this grasp of disciplines should have a certain 'smell' by virtue of which his tastes and professed reactions in describable situations could be fully predicted. It is the aping of this which is sometimes called snobbery.

It is interesting to see how the word came to be given this sense. It has come to acquire this sense, I think, as the result of a process of pauperisation of what the educated man in the seventeenth and eighteenth centuries, the age of enlightenment, stood for. During this period, it was possible for a well-educated man, Leibnitz, for example, to be at once a classicist, a historian, a theologian, a jurist, a mathematician, a physicist, a philosopher, a diplomat, and a politician. That was also the age of the cyclopaedist, the man of universal learning, of whom Diderot was such a refreshing example and Voltaire such a wintry one. It must be acknowledged that the state of development of these disciplines was at that time such that it was possible for one individual to master a number of them in considerable detail. The eighteenth century African philosopher, Antony William

Amo, who lectured in the German universities of Halle, Wittenberg and Jena, published lecture lists in logic, metaphysics, physiology, geomancy, astronomy, theory of codes, and, alas, palmistry. He also mastered history and law. These disciplines have however developed considerably since the eighteenth century. Including palmistry! In the nineteenth century alone the development was awe-inspiring. Many disciplines discovered their true method. In mathematics the idea of rigour firmly set in though it had been broached earlier by Leibnitz, and the appeal to intuition discredited in spite of Kant. It had been thought before, largely under the influence of the German philosopher, Immanuel Kant, that it was possible, and indeed necessary, to appeal to the intuition to sanction mathematical conclusions. Our intuition, he thought, was conditioned by the fact that we were located in time and space. He was therefore uncertain that angels, not being dependant on space and time in the way we with our physical senses were, might not in fact cavil at our mathematical conclusions, or even possibly find them unintelligible. The new rigour divorced mathematics from intuition; and the structure of our senses, while it was naturally important for the ink and paper we used, was made to be irrelevant to mathematical notions and proofs. This was the rout of psychologism in mathematics and indeed logic. Leibnitz's ideas about the relation of logic and mathematics were resurrected. George Boole, an Irishman, and Peano, an Italian, both mathematicians by profession, set to work on showing that mathematics and logic were inter-reducible. Frege and Russell came very near achieving this. The fundamental idea was to be able to distinguish between what could genuinely be proved, and what could not be proved. If you thought a certain proposition enunciated a theorem, you might perhaps set out to prove it; but if you thought it was not a theorem, you could perhaps prove this, but you could not very well produce an unproof of it. There had even been a number of propositions allegedly proved by mathematicians, which turned out to be so far from having been proved that they were quite false. Clearly, if one could invent a method for discriminating more or less mechanically between true general statements and untrue ones, this would be most profitable to a systematic discipline. The attempt to reduce mathematics to logic is the first step towards bringing about this kind of situation in the realm of mathematics.

In the nineteenth century certain disciplines including mathematics found their true method. The consequence of this in the twentieth century is the astonishing progress which has taken place—in the sciences, more than happened in the whole period between the Greeks and the nineteenth century. The kind of development that has taken place is such that to master a science one is called upon to yield to devoted and intensive training of a specialist kind. The concentration of powers required is so complete that the sciences virtually become a closed shop to many other disciplines. This is possibly the source of that divergence which C. P. Snow has called 'the two cultures'. The specialism and visible success of the sciences have nevertheless impressed some minds to such a degree that they have virtually identified the possibilities of human knowledge with the possibilities of science. One indeed finds practitioners of the arts, motivated by the desire to join the scientific bandwagon, resorting to some distressing talk about scientific method in their disciplines. Thus, one has heard of the scientific method in music, painting, literary criticism, history, philosophy. For my part, I should not be surprised to hear people start talking about the scientific method in poetry. Perhaps they have already. There has been a spate of the philosophy of this and the philosophy of that, in an attempt to clarify just what this scientific method consists in for each particular discipline.

The connection of all this with humanism should not be missed. It was remarked earlier on that the idea of the cultured man today is a pauperisation of the cyclopaedist of the age of enlightenment in Europe. This immediately connects it with rational humanism. One may say that the essence of humanism consists in the replacement of God the creator with man the creator. The possibility of doing this is already inherent in the possession of reason, and man's admiration for it. Culture in the age of enlightenment meant cultivation of the reason. Since the sensibilities were held to be subject to the reason, until, and in spite of Hume, who thought that the reason could not recommend any course of action or goal as being worthy of pursuit in itself, ethics and aesthetics were both accepted as being rationalistic. The culmination of this was in Kant's rationalistic ethics, which founded the validity of moral and aesthetic judgments on commands of the reason.

The idea underlying rational humanism is a rational one. It was already involved in Aristotle's account of man as a rational animal and the democratic political theory which he based on this. The idea is that *we* cannot think it accidental that we possess reason. It is true that to flies which thrive on human excrement, the possession of reason by human beings must be a contingent, if for flies a fortunate, matter. But to humans, this is a defining characteristic. This is what should be meant by calling reason a capacity, or a faculty, or a disposition, rather than a sequence of episodic acts. This was the tragedy of Hume. Hume had thought that material objects were simply ideas impressed upon us through sensation. He thought further that each idea was a distinct existence in itself and was unconnected with any other idea. This might be called his atomism. As to the reason itself, he was not quite sure what to say, but inclined towards the position that the reason too was but a bundle of ideas. At this point then two alternatives faced him, either to deny that there was really such a thing as the reason, which he must be deemed to have done, or to say that ideas were themselves percipients. That which perceived was an embarrassment which reduced Hume to speechlessness.

If then we cannot think it accidental that we possess reason, surely it is natural that we should be awed by it. Even when we think it is a rather well-programmed product of evolution, we are unable to avoid being impressed by it. One might further be encouraged to hazard the guess that resorting to stories about well-programmed evolutionary freaks is going back on the idea of evolution. A leap-frogging evolution from one kind to another does not strictly speaking bring sense to the imagination. Leaps and bounds are nothing if they do not abound in hiatuses, and what is a hiatus in this context but an unlegitimised connection? It is incredible that evolution, whether it is conceived to proceed by natural selection (Darwin et al.) or by complexification (Teilhard de Chardin et al.) should from what is not mind produce what is mind. Evolution cannot explain the origin of conscious life.

Now there are two classes of question that one may indeed here pose. Faced with the phenomenon of consciousness and self-consciousness, one can enquire into those conditions which are materially sufficient, that is those physical conditions with which conscious life is associated, e.g. cell-structure, or one can enquire into formally sufficient conditions, that is whatever conditions are the same as the incidence of conscious life. None are known. The identification of the two sorts of condition is responsible for the epi-phenomenalist sort of error which seeks to identify mind with an effect of matter. According to this, mind is but the activity of matter. Here, if you like, is the new animism. If you seek material conditions of thinking, to press the example, physiologists and bio-chemists will tell you about some of the things which go on in the brain when a man thinks. To identify these with thinking is to stand indicted with a *non-sequitur*. The sort of fallacy involved here is identical with that of which Wittgenstein in his *Philosophical Investigations* was guilty, when he treated one's dream as the truthful account that one gave of it. The upshot of his treatment of dreams was in fact to equate the phenomenon of dreaming with the recounting of dreams. That is, a dream becomes in his hand that about it, which is subject to public observation—the account of it. Of mind, it is said that it is that about itself which is subject to public observation, namely, speech and other intelligent activity. The absurdity of the whole procedure is perhaps illustrated in theories of perception. Most theories of perception simply lay down certain physical conditions of perception and then, without further ado, formally identify these conditions with what it consists in to perceive. It may be that I should not see if light did not strike my eyes and an image form on my retina, etc.; but the travelling of light from a source into my eyes, the forming of images on my retina, etc., these cannot, either singly or collectively, be the inwardness of that illumination which is seeing. These physical conditions do not

17

provide an inference to seeing, to consciousness. Indeed, they make perception miraculous.

The degree to which we are infatuated by the idea that we are not contingently rational determines what we are prepared to subordinate to the reason. When this infatuation has reached its white heat, we base ethics, politics, science, and even technology on the sanction of the reason, and empiricism appears in our eyes as the deepest morass of stupidity where people fumble blindly without ideas, and wait to be overtaken by events, rather than distil the essential connection between things through an explication of the ideas of these things. This was Leibnitz's idea. This seventeenth century German genius believed that there was nothing which did not correspond exactly to some idea. The possibilities of occurrences in nature, he thought, were already revealed in the relations of the ideas of things. Hence, to a man who could grasp these ideas and unravel their inner connections there could be no surprises. Empiricism rests on the possibility of surprises, on being wise after the event; but surprises, for Leibnitz, were a psychological condition arising from ignornace and stupidity. It is this kind of Leibnitzian reverence for the reason which leads us to say that we understand God very well, to accuse him of being a mathematician or a rationalist philosopher, or nowadays an economist follower of Ricardo. It is the same kind of Leibnitzian reverence which encourages us to take our fate into our own hands, and write out our own testimonials. The Victorian age in Britain saw the fulfilment of this humanist blasphemy in an emotionally satisfying way. The glories of empire, the wealth of industry and commerce, the martyrised patriotism and long-suffering of the working classes, the formalised perfection of good public etiquette, even the balanced design of the Union Jack, these were all the triumphs of man the creator. Just everything had managed to get formalised, not to say artificialised, and the professed reactions of young ladies, especially, were in any given circumstance completely predictable. It was, however, unbelievable that all this uniformity which formalism brought with it, should have been genuine. The Victorian age, to press the example, consequently continues to languish under a grave suspicion of having been hypocritical. All the same, that self-assured perfectionism, which the Victorian age represented, could not in humanist terms long persist, for humanism is active and militant. What has since happened seems to be a destruction of this perfectionist formalism. As it were, man pulled his perfect creation into smithereens again. This tendency to rip things apart characterises a number of movements in modern Europe. The present atomisation or analysis is not yet complete. The stagnation which arose in the Victorian age and provoked the atomisation, persists in some spheres. The itch towards analysis was indeed already to be felt in the scowling frustration of Dostoievski's Nihilists; and the epidemic of philosophies of all sorts of disciplines is a highlight of the period of stagnation. When someone, instead of getting on with his subject, starts fretting about it, and chats interminably about it, one can be sure that this is not entirely a virtue. The literary critics began to indulge in the philosophy of criticism, the theologians became feverish about the philosophy of religion, and the philosophy of art took precedence over art itself. Even the philosophers, instead of getting on with their philosophy, started wondering about the philosophy of philosophy in a conversational way. Their stagnation-point was reached in the new Philistinism which they called Logical Positivism and Verificationism. At this point, they virtually abandoned philosophy, whose possibility they had really denied by their behaviour, for they saw philosophy as a sort of dictionary of propositions, as distinct from a dictionary of words. In literature the stagnation was reached in the lachrymose sentimentality of poets like Tennyson. In art, it was reached in the syrupy pleasantness and dream-like built-in repose of Impressionism. Impressionism was to art as Mozart was to music. The splitting of the atom by Rutherford in a way became prophetic. In art, Picasso had already pointed at atomism, in dismembering the human body, and putting the bits together again like some nightmare of Empedocles. Peace and calm belong to synthesis. not to analysis. In the post-Victorian analytic age, peace and serenity had already gone. The torture of modern music had already set in, with licentious exploitation of cacophony. In literature succulent imagery gave way to the poetry of the locomotive and of scrap metal. In history, the *Weltanschauung* was being abandoned for Namier's particularism.

As regards man himself, the position was the same. Freud had torn him to shreds, discovering in him not clay in which was encased the living breath of God, but an interweaving of elements imbued with impersonal natures. Motivation and intentionality become in the psychology of Freud the mental analogue of cause and effect. The contrast with Jung is not in the way in which man was broken up, but in the nature of the elements into which he was resolved. Against Freud's impersonality, Jung instituted a limbo of purposeful and often malignant hobgoblins. These two possibilities of atomisation present a double possibility in the account of man after he has been broken up. The two possibilities may be called the essentialist and the scientific. These possibilities are in fact possibilities of reconstruction. And they both concern the nature of man. The one possibility takes an essentialist view of man. This is the possibility opened up by Jung's kind of analysis. It has perhaps been most worked out by the Sartrian species of existentialism. According to an essentialist view of man, there is a constant element in man which is irreducible, and is the essence of being a man. The Sartrian existentialists find this irreducible element in man's alleged ability to act completely without motivation or reason. This kind of belief is also to be encountered in *The Devils* of Dostoievski. If the matter is looked at without bias, one can be permitted to doubt that such an act is possible and believe the Sartrian existentialism to hold that what is most distinctive of man is that he is irrational. The urge to cling to this view of man arises from a disputable belief that what is free cannot at the same time be determined, or have an explanation.

One consequence of this kind of belief is that the reasonable man becomes a slave of his reason, that the pursuit and execution of reasonable acts is so far from representing an enlightened freedom that it is a condemnation to slavery. But if the possession of reason is part of our nature, then we cannot be enslaved by reason, we cannot be enslaved by our nature, for there are no bonds between us and our nature which might be broken. Where there are no bonds, there can be no slavery. Nevertheless, in order that there should be reasonable acts, some form of determinism must be correct. The possibility of planning and producing results depends on the actuality of determinism, on there being sufficient conditions for occurrences.

The Sartrian kind of view would in terms of etiquette idealise the culture of eccentricity. In politics, economics and other departments of state-activity, it would lead to anarchy at normal, and at best to the kind of political and economic individualism put forward by John Stuart Mill. It would tend to minimise the hold of government on people. It would distintegrate culture, and emphasise individualism and eccentricity in all possible spheres. The view of culture that I personally hold is that culture is the common life of the people. It is evident that the essentialist view of humanity that the Sartrian existentialism puts forward cannot be reconciled with the view of culture which I am anxious to defend. But this is not a major source of distress, for whatever culture may not do, at least it puts a bridle on individualism. The Sartrian view should not in fact take kindly to curbs on individualism. Hence it is not consistent with the integrative function of culture.

True as it is that it is in an attempt to spiritualise human nature that the Sartrian existentialism takes an essentialist view of it, there are alternative essentialist views which are not so inconsistent with my view of culture. Indeed the idea of the inevitability of reason to the human condition constitutes an essentialist view of human nature. Essentialist views have themselves changed from era to era. One may even say that it is they which place a *cachet* on their eras. Thus, in the luxuriance of the Greek reason, when the force of generality had been discovered in the time of Thales and before, and people had left rules of thumb in the marshes of the Nile, moving on to proofs and theorems, the new activity of the reason became so impressive both in its contempt for limits and in its winnings, that man was defined as a rational animal. All definitions are, of course, essentialist in import for they identify properties which they hold to be ineluctable. The particular characteristic which the Greeks instituted in their intuition of man led to great achievements in the fields of science and the humanities, in biology, mathematics, logic, philosophy, literature, and political theory. Their technical and artistic achievements were correspondingly great. The fastidiousness involved in intellectual pursuits led them to insist on a certain exactness in practical matters which stood their engineering in good stead. It was the same fastidiousness which elevated their taste in the visible arts. Their sculpture and architecture have haunted European sculpture and architecture down to the beginning of the modern disintegration. But, because the basis of all this was the human reason, which, since it was included in their definition of man, they took every care to develop among themselves, it was possible for their culture to be strongly integrative. Reason is a common property, and was developed along common lines, based on a seriously thought-out theory of education, which was, consequently, in character with them. It was here however that their culture faced its gravest danger. For because reason was susceptible to development, it became natural for Plato to suppose that granted reason was to be the foundation of their society and culture, the most highly developed reasons should hold all power in trust. Descartes stated the other alternative when he insisted that reason was a formal property of man, not a material property, and so it could not vary in degree. The failure of Plato to implement his political theory (in which the dictatorship of the intellectuals was recommended) was at once the triumph of the Athenian democracy. It was what enabled the Athenians to produce that phenomenon, in a relative mode of speech, of effortless unity. Reliance on reason as a defining characteristic of man is nevertheless only one of the ways in which culture can become integrative. The failure of the Sartrian existentialism to inspire such a culture arises solely from the fact that it founds man's nature on irrationality.

But irrationalism is not subject to predictive law, hence it cannot be the spearhead of integration. In any given situation, the possibilities of reasonable response are limited in number. To this extent, the reaction of a reasonable man can be predicted. But when a man is unreasonable, the possibilities of reaction open to him in the same situation are strictly indefinite. They can principally only be limited by his imagination. To Sartrian existentialism therefore culture must be restrictive, and perhaps even intolerable. For it, culture must reduce a man's opportunities of being an individual, because it integrates by normalising, and by placing limits on, the scope of response.

Examples of essentialist views which give rise to integrative cultures are the view of man as the measure of all things, or the view of man as a political animal, or the view of man as an economic animal. Aristotle was somewhat torn between treating man as a rational animal and treating him as a political animal. In the end, he resolved his theoretical anxieties by combining the two, i.e. by saying in effect that man was indeed a political animal, but an animal who was forced by his rationality to seek the one political theory which was rational, that is, a democratic political theory. The view of man as a political animal also obsessed those theorists who made the hypothesis of natural right central to their political philosophy. Locke and Rousseau are cases in point here. The view which is gaining ground in the West and East today is that man is an economic animal. All these views are essentialist, and they generate suitable integrative cultures. The economic view of man is perhaps likely to hold sway in both the West and the East for a long time to come.

Still, an essentialist view of man is not the only possible sort of view which is capable of assuring the integrative aspect of culture. To be clearer about this, one may look a little at the other sort of view, the scientific one. There is a substantial contrast between the two sorts. There is indeed a sense in which even the scientific view of man is essentialist. It is essentialist in the trivial sense that it says minimally that man is necessarily completely predictable in principle. But this is not essentialist in a theoretically interesting way. What is of interest to theory is that in an essentialist view one holds that man's nature cannot be changed in any respect that matters; and it is precisely this which the scientific view of man rejects. The scientific view is not one view, but a kind of view; for scientific accounts may still differ in the elements into which they resolve man. But what is common to them, and significant for culture, is the possibility of changing human nature, the possibility of predicting human reaction with completeness, and so also of planning it. The uses to which such possibilities can be put are obvious. Advertisement and other marketing techniques have profited greatly therefrom. Nor should one ignore the possible significance for both political theory and practice. Especially, if human reactions can be planned, then problems are posed for democracy, which, ideally, thrives on popular consent. Evidently, this consequence of the scientific theory of human nature, which makes it subject to investigation in impersonal and non-valuative terms, and also capable of planning and induced change, has a link with the integrative aspect of culture, culture in fact being here one of the possible ways of expressing homogenised reactions produced through planning and control. The scientific view depends on analysis, disintegration, and then the control of selected variables. It offers the possibility of combining the various elements yielded by the analysis in different ways. It offers various lines of synthesis, each line being an expression of a dominant interest. Sparta, for example, held the scientific view of man, and produced a culture dominated by the military or aggressive interest. Two cultures could not be more opposed than those of Athens and Sparta were. The one was as garrulous as the other was mute. The dominant interest in the synthesis is expressed in what is held constant and what is varied.

The two cultures of C. P. Snow are divided by the essentialist and the scientific views. Those whose study has been in the humanities tend naturally to an essentialist view of man, and those whose study is in the sciences naturally tend to the scientific view. The only way of reconciling them is to discuss the two sorts of views as substantive questions.

The interest in the integrative aspect of culture perhaps calls for explanation. There are at least four things that culture does, and each of them points at culture as an integrative instrument. Society implies a degree of organisation, and the atomistic view of it is contradictory in terms. A collection of unbounded men living poor, nasty, brutish, short, and fearful lives, collected in the mere sense of a plurality, do not form a society. Even a social contract cannot be agreed without some common language, and a common language, the possibility of communication, already stands inconsistent with a group in which every man behaved as though he were author of himself and knew no other kin. For the purposes of organising society there are broadly speaking two views about what may form the foundation. These views in a way coincide with the essentialist and the scientific contrast. For society can be regarded as founded on a system of rights or as founded on a system of duties. When society is held to be founded on rights, one can expect some doctrine of natural rights with which every individual is born, and which cannot be alienated from him. This kind of view is usually based on philosophy or religion or a mixture of the two. John Locke, for example, held that if a man mixed a portion of a common with the labours of his own body, he had created a property in the common. Property is to be understood here as entailing the exclusive right of use. Locke's idea is based on philosophical peculiarities of the first person. The peculiarity can be illustrated by the following exercise. If I scratch the back of my head, and challenge you to do the same, there are two alternatives facing you, and against either I may well raise objections. If you scratch the back of your head, I can cavil that I scratched the back of *my* head, but you are scratching the back of *your* head. If you scratch the back of my head, I can complain that I scratched the back of my own head, but you are scratching the back of someone else's head. The stage is now set for Locke to say that the first person is unique, only I am I, and its properties are inalienable. And the declension through the nominative to the ablative cannot affect this. The labours of my body, even in the genitive, are the labours of *my* body, and cannot be shared. Anyone who bases the notion of private property on this peculiarity of the first person is operating the view of society as founded on rights. Society becomes atomistic, and it becomes inessential to the human condition that it is situated in society. The function of government in such a view becomes largely the reconciliation and defence of multiple rights. That is, one begins with John Locke and ends up with

John Stuart Mill or one begins with Rousseau and ends up with some form of existentialist political thesis.

If society is thought on the other hand to be founded on a system of duties, the function of government becomes largely one of resolving conflicts of duties, for duties as well as rights give rise to conflicts among one another. The foundation of a society on a network of duties at once excludes the atomism of that society. The difference between duties and rights as the foundation of society, though at first theoretical, in fact has practical issue in the types of institutions which can be regarded as acceptable. The question of the choice of institutions is not a purely theoretical one, but has also a practical admixture; it is in the end a choice between practical alternatives. When the solution of a problematic situation is based on general ideas about the nature of society, the solution is still not an implicate of the problems. When stated largely enough, these problems admit of a variety of theoretically possible solutions. But the particular solution that proves successful depends on the emphasis that has been given to certain aspects of culture. The Western view of society, for example, makes certain specified rights antecedent to the organisation of society. But it should be seen that the catalogue of antecedent rights may vary according to the kind of foundation which one proposes to rest them on. Where duty is explainable in terms of the safeguarding of rights, rights of personal property will be quite fundamental, and the institutions of the society will have an over-riding regard to this. Where duty is not explainable in terms of keeping the peace between rights, that is, where the *raison d'etre* of duties is not the safeguarding of rights, being in a society becomes recognised as essential to the human condition. Society becomes antecedent to rights, not rights to society.

But whether society is seen as based on rights or duties, it is still clear that a considerable portion of the life of the people falls outside governmental interference and action, and, properly, even interest. What a government does in terms of the life of any individual is to place limits on his possibility of action, but as far as the range of his free action goes, a government does little more than to highlight certain possibilities. This it does most often by assuring that opportunities of such choices are protected and underlined. Through educational programmes, for example, every government underlines certain opportunities whether in the civil service, in industry, or in teaching. But though it is only a fragment of the possible actions of any individual that can be controlled by direct state intervention, however alert and purposeful, it is essential, if individuals live in a community, that individual action should not become too bizarre. The possibility of state intervention itself depends on the co-operation of individuals, and this co-operation implies appreciable unity of purpose. Every individual depends for his life and living on the sufferance and co-operation of others, but the less people find it natural to feel that the other man depends for his continuance on their private sufferance and co-operation, the less is the chance of this sufferance and co-operation being withheld. Culture is an instrument for making the sufferance and co-operation natural. Its success depends on the extent to which it is allowed to be self-authenticating. Though it allows for internal discussion, and is indeed nourished thereby, the principles of decision in such discussions are themselves provided by the culture. By uniting the people in common beliefs and attitudes, or at least, in tolerance for certain beliefs, actions and values, culture fills with order that portion of life which lies beyond the pale of state intervention.

A second aspect of culture connected with the above arises from the way in which it fills that portion of life which is not subject to state intervention. It fills it in such a way as at the same time to integrate its society, on the basis of common reactions, common actions, common interests, common attitudes, common values. It creates the basis of the formulation of a common destiny and cooperation in pursuing it. If one looks at the West one finds that this use of culture is well-developed. It is what is involved, when one hears it said that this or that belief will destroy a certain way of life, and that that way of life must be defended no matter what the cost. In socialist countries, the same aspect of culture is being quickly developed in appeals to the socialist conscience in order to destroy certain social ills including hooliganism. What one society says for itself, another society may say of itself.

A third use of culture is to make events intelligible and significant. National problems arise in the context of the national situation. And they derive their significance, they become critical, only in the empyrean glow that the circumvenient culture disengages on them. Any effective and lasting solution must take its elements from national resources. To sift, to pick, and to synthesise in critical situations, one needs an idea or a cluster of over-riding ideas, and the culture is the repertoire of just these ideas and techniques and attitudes, the spring of effort, which the people understand and with which they are able to cope, and have lived. The same event has varying significance in different cultural settings. Chipping a coronation stone in Britain and in 19th century Ashanti would bring different retribution. It would have brought death in Ashanti. The difference in severity of the retribution can only be explained by a difference in the position of something like a coronation stone in the two cultures. History is always the light that some culture throws on events. And it is the determining power of culture which makes prophecy possible in history. When a people have a common culture, the significance thrown on events finds substantial acceptance, and the policy called into being to cope with them has the chance of authenticity. The ideals of two different cultures may themselves be different. And if ideals can be distinguished from the institutions which make them effective at all, then even when two cultures share common ideals the institutions expressing these ideals may still be different. The relation between ideals and institutions is not one of identity, and when institutions are effective, the whole reason for this cannot be because they express and fortify certain ideals. The success of institutions depends on local conditions and resources and as these change significantly, political theory recommends adjustments in institutions. The necessity for institutional changes is itself an expression of the need to preserve ideals. The realisation that the same ideals can be served by differing institutions, and that institutions are so to say idiomatic, is one that Africa and Asia can bring home to Europe. This realisation also reveals that political theory, in so far as it deals with institutions, is quite relative, and by no means to be assumed in any given instance to be simply universal in its applicability.

A fourth aspect of culture is to control change. This is a corollary of what has gone before. There is no doubt that processes of industralisation, for example, initiate cultural change. They lead to urbanisation, to the mass movement of labour from the country to the cities, to the break-up of those silent connections which make the family and the fellowship of rural life. They tend to replace a sense of community with a sense of individualism, because in the urban situation one's powers are continually taxed, and merit and success are individual. New problems of what one does with leisure arise because the setting of leisure is new. The strength of culture controls the extent to which disruptive forces have free and successful play. It is possible for the purpose of discussing this fourth aspect of culture to think of culture as comprising three facets: material, including property systems and technology; institutional, including customs and ritual as well as more obviously political and social institutions; and finally value, including ethics, religion, and literature and art to the extent that these include aspirations or judgment. It is the material aspect of culture which is today subject to the most relentless change. The appurtenances of industrialised communities, items like cars, and other consumer luxuries have firmly entrenched themselves in the lives of African communities which are in no sense industrialised. In Africa, these luxuries of material culture are not benefits of industrialisation as they are elsewhere, but antecedents of it, though certain techniques, like those of communication and, to a smaller extent, of production, have already been taken over there. But it is instructive to enquire whether this expansion and change in the material culture of Africa has in any way nibbled at the institutional and value structures. Has material culture expanded without reference to either of the other two aspects? And even if the other two aspects have seen modifications, possibly pauperisation, as material culture has expanded, is this through some internal connection, or is it purely *laissez-faire*? It will probably be found that the other two aspects of culture have suffered in Africa at the same time as the material culture has yielded to Western seductions. Social institutions have changed considerably. Class differentiations have become much more fluid than they ever were before, and social mobility is considerable. This seems to be an effect of expanding material culture everywhere, especially when this expansion is the result of industrialisation. Rank and prestige come to be associated with the possession of particular skills or the enjoyment of a minimum level of affluence. The symbols of prestige and class are not what they used to be. Groups of merchants have come to the fore, and have made such an impression through what they can command, that to associate them with a high class it is no longer thought necessary to enquire into their origins. The educational system which has come along with the expansion in material culture has created groups of individuals who were indispensable to the colonial administration, and so were seen, in the period of the loss of independence, to be associated with the new sources of power. The gap between these groups and the vast mass of the population which is still largely agricultural or employed in unskilled occupations, or semi-skilled occupations, is considerable and is underlined by the virtual absence of a bridging middle-class. And countless numbers of those who according to the traditional reckoning would be held to be of a high class become irrelevant. The traditional reckoning is nevertheless not defunct, but is also contemporary. For something like ninety per cent of Africa must surely be traditional. This is indeed a measure of the difference between the towns and the villages. The new élite concentrate in the towns, and the old élite continue what in national terms must be regarded as a sort of suspended animation in the villages. The inequalities between the towns and the villages are bound to increase in the early stages of industrialisation, for at this time, the industrial process must be cruelly selective, and the necessary infra-structure has most obvious fulfilment in the towns. Great drainage of population will be exerted on the villages through migrant labour; and unless communications in the form of good roads linking villages to towns are quickly developed, the villages will be atrophied even of that comparative rejuvenation which arises from constant trafficking with the nation's nerve-centres. It is quite possible, however, that the traditional system of ranking people may to some extent mitigate, modify, or even attenuate some of the rather profound cleavages and differences in opportunities which have already emerged. But this rather depends on cultural education. One can say, however, that traditional class systems in Africa have not had such a blasting effect on social relations as they have done in the West and the East. This is a question which will be gone into in the next chapter. Suffice it to say here that it appears that through judicious grafting, one may avoid some of the excesses which have been associated with a lopsided expansion of material culture in Europe. A class struggle as such has no meaning in terms of African culture. The conditions for its arising as a question are not even given.

It may be said that the expansion of material culture has made for social mobility, for relative ease in movement from one class to another. There is a sense too in which the traditional system of ranking may be said to allow for social mobility. If class is linked with authority and leadership, then the traditional system is certainly open to social mobility. It is, however, more correct to say that in the traditional system class was purely descriptive and carried no necessary implications about function, power, or authority. In this sense, it allowed for no mobility. One was born into a class, grew up in it, and died in it. Europe seems to be moving towards this in its former aspect today. For being a nobleman in Europe does not appear today to carry any necessary implication of function, power or authority. The traditional African system allowed for even slaves to become leaders, inasmuch as questions of function, power and authority related to specialisms. As long as no specialism was involved, one's class might give one precedence, especially in processions and kindred matters. But when specialisms were involved like statecraft and wisdom, there was nothing analogous to primogeniture. It was possible for a slave who distinguished himself in wisdom and the knowledge of statecraft to acquire a position of leadership and authority without revolution.

The institution of the family too has received some rude shocks. In many cases it is in practice no longer the very closely-knit web that it was. Responsibilities have been narrowed now in response to economic pressures. This sort of response in fact stands condemned in the traditional value system. When one is asked within the framework of traditional values whether one's greed for money is so great that one is prepared to see one's kin perish, one gathers the impression that one is being asked an ultimate, almost rhetorical question. But the new standard of living consequent on the increased consumption of an expanding material culture does not allow every meal to become a feast for countless demanding mouths. So one treasured value becomes jeopardised. To the extent that the obligations enjoined by this value are ignored, to that extent society is on the way to atomism. The family steadily contracts into man, wife, and children.

The institution of chiefship too suffers some weakening. The nation has now become a unit in Africa, where the tribe was a unit. The territory of the nation is far larger than that of any tribe. This, of course, immediately affects the institution of chiefship. Paramount chiefs are no longer sovereign chiefs, and they are compelled to have relations within certain regional Councils with neighbouring chiefs. This itself is an expression of nationhood, and is paralleled at the ordinary level by considerable movement of citizens in jurisdictions of other chiefs. Labour movements alone have effectively corroded the grasp and hold that the traditional chief had over his own people. And in any case, with his ceasing to be sovereign, and the focus of power and source of politic decisions, his people have quickly ceased to look up to him for direction. He became more a social figure than a political one, but even the pageantry that belonged to him in this watered-down role is little in evidence to-day. To-day, the chief is not even always a first-class citizen. And by the time that industrialisation has fully set in in Africa, no single tribe can provide or can be allowed to provide the massive labour that will be involved. Part of the traditional

32

authority of sovereign-like chiefs has to be in abeyance to free the labour needed for substantial industrialisation. With larger groupings of people, the tendency is for the basis of tribal groupings and chiefs to be weakened, and for smaller groupings to transform themselves into even smaller and less effective ones in the form of clubs and other societies. At the same time, since a lot of culture in Africa is tied up with tribal groupings, the question of preservation will quickly arise for culture, the need to devise new institutions to embrace some of the older aspects involved in culture. And this is an exercise in values.

The value aspect of culture is well able to place sanctions and embargoes on material culture and institutional culture. It has been pointed out that every age has a certain picture of man, of what he essentially is, and so of what the good for him is. When the idea of him being operated is that man is an economic animal, no further justification is required for submerging other human interests to the economic interest. But even so, the desirability of development and of the satisfaction of the economic interest would still be part of the value aspect of the culture of the people. That the desirability of this would be part of the value aspect of culture is much clearer where man is not held primarily to be an economic animal. In the West as in vast tracts of the East, the current doctrine of man is that he is an economic animal. The two areas have their own contending intuitions of the one economic doctrine which value culture in the light of this definition of man is supposed to hallow. In the West, the intuition yields capitalistic theories, in the East Marxist. Both sides stand poised to defend the veracity of their intuition, their particular economic doctrine, and, especially, practice.

The interrelation between the three aspects of culture can be found everywhere. The interrelation may even be illustrated in the following manner. When one culture borrows some of its industrial technique and institutions from another culture, one can expect that, depending on how central these are in the matrix, they will already be controlled and permeated with other cultural elements, even if these only take the form of tea breaks. It could certainly happen that these borrowed items are in their

33

native setting surrounded by ideals, attitudes, relationships, inter-human habits, which include design of buildings, amenities, types and method of control of labour, relationships between employees and managers and employers, attitudes of labour to work, and happen to be repeated in their new setting. But even when this is so, the borrowers may still feel considerable pain at their own institutions and techniques having been replaced. This is sometimes due to the mistaken but natural belief that the new institutions cannot be serving the same purpose writ large, or are not informed by the same ideals. But this belief, though sometimes mistaken, has an opportunity of being correct from the very fact that it is natural. Indeed, that this is a distinct possibility is a consequence of the corrosive effect of material culture on the value aspect of culture. The possibility that certain techniques and institutions are already infused with cultural elements of the people from whom they are lifted, may well make it impossible to effect a simple transplantation. It may become necessary to carry out an operation more in the nature of a graft. The ease with which they can be grafted on to a new culture depends on how alien to the other culture the second culture is in terms of value aspects.

With the above sketch of the integrative powers of culture, I feel free to go back to the two sorts of view of man. In spite of thinkers like Sartre, the view of man which is gaining ground in the West today is the scientific view, the view that in theory nothing that man can do is surprising, that everything can be foreseen. This is borne out by the treatment of such ideas as those of democracy as a purely sociological phenomenon, e.g. in a recent book by Martin Lipset, called *Political Man*. The point was made earlier on that the scientific analysis of man offered alternatives of synthesis, each line of synthesis being dominated by some over-riding interest. What the scientific analysis does not cope with is the apparent possibility of choice or decision on the dominant interest. Each line of synthesis is accompanied by a culture which is appropriate and congenial to it. That synthesis of man which makes him out to be an economic animal is accompanied by a culture which has marked tropisms towards consumption and materialism. And this brings East and West together in spite of the feeble or hysterical, seldom sober and serious, murmurings about God and spirit that the West sporadically works up. It was also suggested that the West was in a sort of turmoil of analysis, and was not well on the way to synthesising the elements of man again. If the full acceptable synthesis of man is compared to the paradisiac state, as the Victorian age in Britain might well have been, then the present preoccupation with the economic man reflects a determination to enjoy the good things of this world while waiting for those of the next. The East differs from the West in its approach to paradise. The syndromes are similar, except that in the East the blueprint of paradise seems already to have been worked out to the satisfaction of the East.

But what shall Africa, which is not of the West or of the East, do? It would perhaps at least be an act of supine madness to ape the West or the East, indeed any point of the compass, like a new sun-worship, in ways which cannot leave the cultures of Africa the same without our having an interest in what is dominant in the external culture, or without bothering to understand its mechanics and rationale. This only leads to periodic and violent regurgitation as it has done in Singapore where the government has been in the throes of a reactionary and puritanic crusade in morals. Here is a question of policy.

In newly independent Africa, the period of the loss of independence entailed a certain measure of deculturisation which was mercifully not complete. It was also a period of ineffectuality for the cultures of Africa, a period of cultural dislocation and lack of purpose, because the new visible sources of power, and the springs of decision, had no reference to the local culture. In areas where the local culture was not contiguous with the new forces, this has meant a sort of suspended animation for it. The cleavage between town life and village life was complete. This in itself would have been sufficient to prevent the deculturisation from being widespread. But added to this must be the fact that the purposes of the deculturisation did not refer to Africa, but were oriented towards the needs of Europe. Educated persons who were personally successful were so oriented to the extent to which they identified themselves with the new, but alien culture. One finds a mushrooming of ladies' societies in which some of the regulations were that the African ladies should neither speak African languages nor wear African clothing. Salvation and refinement consisted in an assiduous, if imperfect, cultivation of European manners and modes. This was the effect of being contiguous with the new European culture. It was less alien, however, and so made less havoc, in places like the north of Nigeria where the deep Moslem commitment emphasised a superb aristocratic bearing, a poise of attitude which the nineteenth century British pro-consuls in Africa understood and found to their liking.

It is important to stress the traditional nature of Africa. Some ninety per cent of independent Africa must be accounted to be traditional. In the period of the loss of independence, this large majority did not share a culture which had any constructive place in the planning of policies, and in their authentication. This large majority was therefore unable to feel involved in what went on. Therefore when leadership came to them it was easy to bring to the fore the deep-seated feeling of being at a loss or even of being frustrated. It was an increasingly natural question to say: but who is this white man who tells us what to do and what not to do, whom I serve, and who tells me what is good for us? Is the white man one of us? This sort of question had brought about periods of sporadic social and political unrest as early as the nineteenth century. Africa was nationalistic at the time that Europe was, and nationalism in Africa is not a twentieth century European bequest as many Europeans still think. This kind of thought is a failure to recognise what has struck one. Not to see the blow coming is sometimes understandable, but to fail to see what has struck one, even when the blow has been received, betrays a serious defect in adjustment. The regaining of political independence quickly appeared as a condition of reinstituting the culture which is understood and which one has learnt to work. Culture is the instrument of that segmented integration which is the basis of national involvement. The twentieth century phenomenon in Africa is the emergence of a number of truly great political parties. The realisation of the securing of political independence as an indispensable condition of coming into one's own, of the making relevant of a people's culture to national processes, was perhaps first given explicit force by the Convention People's Party, Ghana's ruling party. Even when political affiliation follows ethnic and sub-ethnic lines, the binding force is identity of cultural range. When ethnic and sub-ethnic groups conjoin in a common political organisation, identity of objective is a binding force, but not a crucial one. One hears it said every other day that opposition to foreign domination is almost exclusively that which brings about a unity in political movements in Africa, and this unity, it is said, is but contingent and limited. This exclusive role of opposition to foreign rule would lead one to expect the political parties to fall apart as soon as independence is attained. This does not seem to have happened in general. The truly national parties have not broken up and fallen apart in Africa any more than they did in India with the coming of independence. It is to the divisive elements in cultures which exist next to each other that one must turn. In the Congo, where the Balubas have an articulate philosophy to hold their culture together in strong contrast to the surrounding groups, the Balubas have played a role which, while disintegrative of the Congo, is at the same time consolidatory of them. There is a distinct connection between the areas of regional culture and local or district government.

I wish to put forward culture as that knock-down rhetoric by means of which political objectives are sold. In Britain, I suspect that this has been a discovery of the Conservative Party, and it has probably been their chief instrument in stemming the rise of the Labour Party. The Labour Party of Britain in terms of proportion of population in fact has its greatest support to-day. A great deal of this support appears, however, to stem from a vision of it, while the Conservatives are in power, as a source of economic advance, for in industrial disputes it could be predicted where the sympathies of an Opposition Labour Party might lie. This utilitarian affiliation to the Labour Party is itself, so to say, compelled by the mass assault of some type of material culture which the newspapers, television, and advertising agencies have felt free to foster under Conservative patronage. The stirrings of the Labour Party's interest in culture today could be an attempt to give the present engrossment in mass culture a new direction, such that the achievement of that culture would not be seen as consisting in voting a Tory party into power and then wringing prizes from it.

Because the vast majority of our populations are still traditional, politicians and statesmen of Africa have a clear choice before them: whether to be as alien to their own people as the colonial government has been, to complete the deculturisation which set in, and to substitute in Africa some new effective culture which has no roots in Africa, or whether to pose problems, to formulate ideals and national objectives meaningfully in terms of the cultures of Africa, which have in fact continued to be in force.

Culturally speaking, a newly independent country is full of broken ends, and the cultural strings have to be mended. The problems inherent in the mending of the strings would be common to the newly-independent countries, but their particular formulation would have to respond to cultural bias. For the purposes of enthusiastic reconstruction, even willing reconstruction, particular cultural patterns have to be deepened and also spread. Methods of cultural education, including open discussion, will themselves depend on the level and the extent of the consciousness of the unleashing culture.

The politicians and statesmen of Africa have in their public utterances recognised the relevance of African cultures to the process of reconstruction. In the preoccupation with the African personality they appear to hold that the guiding principles of the future of Africa will be those authenticated in the African experience and cultures. Progress, its objectives, and some of its avenues are thought of in terms of a picture of the African personality. In a way, it is obvious that it is the cultures of the people which will determine what aspects of the Western civilisation, or the Middle Eastern, are retained, what aspects modified, what aspects discarded. These choices do not happen gratuitously and without reason, but rest squarely on those silent adjustments which have their nerve-centres in the heritage of the people. The recognition of the relevance of the African personality, namely, that complex of ideas and attitudes which is both identical and significant in otherwise different African cultures, makes it necessary to find out just in what this corpus of ideas and attitudes, at once identical and significant, consists, and by confrontation to find out very clearly what we need to borrow and the possibility of integrating it with our own cultures, indeed to find out also what we shall not be too grieved to discard in our own culture.

At the same time, one does not wish the traditional cultures of Africa to be too constricting, to exert a stranglehold on our future. What makes our traditional cultures significant is the fact that they are also contemporary. But present with them in Africa today are some digested Western elements, and some undigested ones; and also certain Middle Eastern elements associated with the Islamic religion, which have found fertile soil in Africa. The point of a culture which I have been dwelling on is that it is the source of solidarity, of the complex mechanisms, symbols, and ideologies of social integration and common belongingness; if you like, the living being of a nation. National-building requires that more parochial allegiances like tribal ones should not take up a strong and hostile posture. The cultural elements which I have mentioned are all present in African countries, and have to be taken into account in any synthesis. If God made man, God did not at the same time create culture. Culture is not biological, but is entirely of man's making. Its content at all levels and at all times depends on mental bent and other prevailing conditions.

Attempts have for some time been made to represent Africa as a sort of colossal *tabula rasa*, blank sheet, where culture is concerned. It is said that all Sudanese peoples, that is black peoples, owe their state organisation, religion, and much of their material culture to non-negro sources, usually ancient Egyptian. Starting with this as premise when it should be their conclusion, some anthropologists have felt justified in being concerned with the history of Africa. This preoccupation seems to depend on two opinions held by some of them. First there is the view that while other continents have for a long time shaped history, Africa has been enmeshed in a sort of a-historical morass; it has only recently broken upon history. Its history, as it were, happened to it. There is also the view that the genuine Africa, the Africa of the man in the bush, is so near to pure nature that in Africa one beholds humanity virtually in its infancy. Now anthropologists sometimes call their discipline a science, though the opportunities of experiment are non-existent. If one, however, makes the assumption that there is a common history of ideas by which all mankind live, then by juxtaposing Africa to other peoples who have climbed higher in the historical tree of ideas, one is offered a satisfying substitute for experiment, a sort of margarine for butter. It hardly need be said that the more discerning anthropologists do not sub-scribe to this. Among a people who have no tradition of recorded history, anthropology is indeed important to the reconstruction of pre-literate history. But what social anthropology does is roughly to analyse culture and place its elements together in such a way that significant elements appear significant. This kind of concern can explain internal changes in a society, but it cannot guarantee a historical conclusion as to the origins of the culture involved. For historical conclusions historical evidence is required.

If one takes Mrs Meyerowitz's substantial work on the Akans of Ghana as an example, then it quickly becomes evident that she has not felt any necessity for bringing forward distinctly historical evidence. And even if one takes her work at the level of speculative history, the feeling of dissatisfaction with it continues.

Mrs Meyerowitz compares Akan ideas about the divine kingship and the religious, political and social institutions which the Akans associate with it, with similar aspects of different periods of Ancient Egypt. On the strength of this, she proceeds to say that the Akans trace these ideas and institutions, as well as their political organisation and much of their material culture, to the ancient Egyptians. An impressive pedigree, but utterly unsupported by anything like the kind of historical evidence called for. In particular, she does not try very hard to show that the ancient Akans ever lived in ancient Egypt or in areas independently known to have been previously dominated by

the ancient Egyptians. Taking her work at the level of speculative history, one finds that the ideas and institutions involved
are intellectual ones, not questions of rule of thumb. They were
fundamental to the ancient Egyptian polity, as to the Bono-
Tekyiman polity. They would not have been common knowledge among the ancient Egyptians any more than they are
among the Akans. They were in fact buried in the secrets of
ancient Egyptian writing, and the priests would have been their
monitors. A people who had access to these ideas to the extent
of the detail claimed by Mrs Meyerowitz would have been
bound to borrow the art of writing as well, if they had not
obtained it already. It is rather disappointing therefore that
Mrs Meyerowitz makes little attempt to explain the absence of a
system of writing among the Akans. The quality of borrowing
claimed is comparable to the Western indebtedness to the
Graeco-Roman civilisation. This involves concepts of law,
religious ritual, social and political theory and organisation.
But the West, one notes, has not failed to be involved with
concomitant questions. The system of writing has been taken
over. Linguistic influence is in evidence. Artistic conception
and execution, and the calendar, have been copied. Even in
Africa today, where the quality of the borrowing from Europe
is less than Mrs Meyerowitz claims for the Akans *vis-à-vis* the
ancient Egyptians, one finds that these other things have been
taken over with what is called the *Pax Britannica* or, I suppose,
the *Pax Gallica*. Religious ideas and art go together because
one has to represent the pantheon and design ritual. These are
not questions which are windowless on one another. Hence
when Mrs Meyerowitz says as regards the calendar that she has
not written a book about ancient Egyptian influences in general,
and as regards art that she agrees that Akan art has a distinctive
quality of its own, the sense of dismay becomes acute.

If the culture of the Akans is really almost wholly ancient
Egyptian in origin, one expects a great deal of the Akan vocabulary to be ancient Egyptian. Mrs Meyerowitz, leaning rather
heavily here on L. Homburger, alleges that all negro African
languages, on account of numerous common elements, have
their origin in that of ancient Egypt. The negro African

languages have few visible common elements as things are. To talk not only of numerous common elements among them, but also between them and ancient Egyptian, is to break even the gossamer laws of fantasy. But L. Homburger, set up though she is by Mrs Meyerowitz as her authority, writes with less alertness than her disciple. Whereas Mrs Meyerowitz has in fact tried to work out, in considerable detail, a hypothesis which has been broached for all Sudanese peoples, Homburger for her part seems bent on conglomeration. She is struck by the Fula hump-backed cattle and, without further ado, surmises that they are of Dravidian origin. She notices the incidence of glottal stops and says that Fula must come from Sindi of North-West India. She takes little account of sound-shifts which are everywhere crucial in linguistic classification.

What Jan-Heinz Jahn does in his book *Muntu* is the obverse of Mrs Meyerowitz's work. But whereas one can only say that her work is not sufficiently alert, his work does not respond at all to depth soundings. It is best described as a piece of journalism. His idea of African culture is of a mixture of the Western suavity of Senghor and anything which African politicians and other men of influence may choose to believe of their own past, for, Jahn says, what they believe is what is effective, and for this reason alone must be true, not in any sense of being connected with evidence, but simply because it has been said. Overtly, Jahn's work has thrusting airs of being sympathetic, but of the two works, his is undoubtedly the more pernicious. His contempt for the reality of the traditional African culture as a historical fact is reproduced when he writes of African literature. He lumps meritorious poems and trash together without comment, and as equal evidence of African literature.

I believe that there is a *type* of African culture, and that this type is essentialist in inspiration. The essentialist view of man underlying this type finds expression in the art, the ethics and morality, the literary and the religious traditions, and also the social traditions of the people. African society is in type rationalistic. Principles to guide the solutions of human problems are always forthcoming, clear and bold. Our interest in our own cultures is not historical or archaeological, but directed towards the future. It helps importantly in solving the question not what Africans were like, but how we can make the best of our present human resources, which are largely traditional. This emphasis makes the development of African cultural education not only theoretically but also pragmatically satisfying.

The development of cultural education calls, however, for tremendous and widespread effort. This effort will be geared to moulding our cultures into something articulate in a literate way to meet the challenges of the modern world.

The cultural alienation which makes the focus on our culture necessary has gone down even to our primary schools. The folk-tales our children were told were other people's folk-tales, not ours. The standards of passable behaviour, possible ideals and aspirations put forward in these tales could not always be assumed to be ours.

Cultures, I have suggested, are linked with an essentialist or a scientific view of human nature. Our culture is, I believe, linked with an essentialist view. I have so far suggested that events of large significance take place within the setting of some culture, and take their significance from the culture in which they find themselves. The value aspect of culture appears to be the dominant aspect, for cultural progress implies selection and rejection, and this implies subjection to values. When one people borrows from another people, culture becomes relevant, for one is liable to take over inessentials along with what there is a genuine need to take over. I have also endeavoured to emphasise the integrative function of culture. And this aspect of it is, I think, enough to excite the interest of Africans in their own cultures. It must be emphasised however that the interest is not a historical or an archaeological one merely, though even that is engaging enough. It is in fact directed towards the future, for it helps in solving the question, not what we were like centuries ago, but how the best can be made of our present human resources. This emphasis makes the development of African cultural education not only theoretically but also pragmatically satisfying.

CHAPTER 2

PARADIGM OF AFRICAN SOCIETY

Similarity between Cultures—Paradigm of African culture—Its philosophical aspect—Its supernatural aspect—Its theory of man and society—Its theory of government—Its legal system—Its military organisation—Its literature—Its ethics and metaphysics—Institutions and theory.

EACH CULTURE, WHILE REMAINING the same, passes through different successive *milieux*, phases. Each culture has a number of basic aspects each of which has the possibility of becoming dominant. A *milieu* or phase of a culture is determined by that aspect of the culture to which greatest emphasis is currently given, while the other aspects are kept in mild abeyance. This possibility of a culture, which passes through a succession of *milieux* or phases, nevertheless remaining the same is that which enables one to give a certain kind of account of the culture. This kind of account is correct in its own way, though hardly reflecting any particular phase of the culture. The possibility of so presenting a culture is the possibility of putting forward its framework, the range within which each phase of it is set. Much controversy about culture in fact boils down to a discussion in favour of this or that phase of the culture. Thus, one might say that F. R. Leavis would like the puritanic streak in British culture to become dominant at this moment, to become thematic of it. If the puritanic element should become dominant, one could then say of British culture that it had entered its puritanic phase or *milieu*. The totality of streaks, which limits the possibility of phases, is all there all the time, and there is an abiding open possibility of any one of the streaks becoming dominant, thematic. It is like the legs of an insect; they are all there, but the insect can be picked up by a different leg each time.

In this chapter I shall attempt to present what I grasp to be the typical range of African cultures. The central feature of the type to which African cultures belong is that there is a certain world-view to which can be related all other central concepts, including those of religion and theology, morality and social organisation. I therefore propose to give some account of this world-view, and to illustrate the way in which all other central aspects of the traditional African society flow from it. In order to do this, I shall choose a given African society. My paradigm will be the Akan of Ghana.

The Akan of Ghana represent some two-thirds of the six and a half million people of Ghana. They are to be found in Ashanti and to the south, and in Axim and to just west of Accra. They speak a cluster of languages which have a family resemblance but are not related as language to dialect.

In introducing the idea of a paradigm, it is not my intention to suggest that all African cultures, or even the majority of them, share a certain identity of principles and a certain identity of detail. Every culture has its sanctions. It is these sanctions which indicate what general value statements are within that culture reasonable. Such general value statements affect law, ethics and social organisation. And they are commonly held to be incapable of non-circular proof. Even in a Kantian sort of framework, in which general normative principles are founded on edicts of the reason, sooner or later one reaches practical principles which are held to be imposed by reason upon itself. Elsewhere, it can only be with reference to individual cultures that these general value statements are held to become reasonable or valid.

It is of course possible for two cultures to share the same general values. Where this happens, the institutions expressing the values could still be different from place to place. And each of the cultures would also have several cultural phenomena which will not be directly linked with any particular general values. This section of a culture, which includes the phenomena not directly linked with any particular general values, may be

referred to as the mannerisms of the culture. In that case where
two cultures share the same inspiration, their mannerisms may
still be different. Mannerisms would most obviously include
those objects which are subject to taste. Indeed, the cobwebby
saying 'de gustibus non est disputandum' may itself be said to be a
confession that tastes, in so far as they are mannerisms of a
culture, are not directly linked with its higher general values.
Nevertheless, tastes lend themselves to use as auxiliary devices
for supporting a cultural phase or milieu.

So far it has been suggested how instances of the same type-
culture may differ. But one also expects resemblances between
them. The resemblances are, however, not the kind which one,
so to say, finds between sentences of different languages expressing the same thought. Cultures which belong to the same
type could still be in different milieux or phases. Their
mannerisms could be different; and so more obviously could
their institutions be. The resemblances between cultures of the
same type are rather to be thought of in terms of family likeness.
Here the same culture could markedly resemble different
cultures of the same type in different ways—like the members
of a family.

This is what justifies the substantial treatment of an individual culture treated as paradigmatic of a type. It would be
unsatisfactory to attempt to present the schema of the type itself.

The Akan thought very much about the world, not, indeed,
as the world inside which he found himself, but as the world of
which he formed a part. The Akan did not have an attitude of
externality to the world. For him the world was metaphysical,
not scientific. Properly to understand this view, it is necessary
to think that modernity consists in the assassination of ideas,
in the whittling down of the extent to which the conception
of the relations between ideas determines the content and nature
of the world. In Europe this is now held to be possible only in
the field of thought and action. In Europe, the world is for the
rest hardly an intellectual world; and it is of the essence of
research, for example, that whoever made the world was not a
rationalist philosopher.

According to the Akan's metaphysical view, the world is

rationalist philosophical. Relations between ideas take on body and flesh in the relations between things in nature. According to such a view, therefore, the true metaphysics must be a deductive system. And morality, politics, medicine are all made to flow from metaphysics. From this point of view, science with its experimentalism becomes a simulation of stupidity.

With the growth of science and technology in Europe the scope of morality as the implicate of metaphysics has dwindled; one finds morality yielding to medicine, the relation between thought and action giving ground to that between cause and effect, by way of motives and childhood antecedents. Evil-doers and sinners masquerade as sick men and invalids. But to the Akan, the distinction between wrong and sin was hardly there, the same word, *ebon*, casting the same kind of gloom over wrongs and sins. It is as though instead of wrong and sin, one used the word, evil. Sin was the counterpart in human activity of contradiction in human thinking. Since contradiction paralyses thought, it follows that sin or evil would be heavily punished. Since metaphysics spewed out morality, politics, medicine, theory of social organisation, *et cetera*, the consequences of an error in metaphysics could well be grave. And this is possibly that which explains that severity of punishment among the Akans which has appeared as barbarity. What the growth of science does is to anthropologise morality and politics. Morality comes to be based on that complex which suits men in their present circumstances, or on the consensus of human opinion. A sort of utilitarianism and naturalism in ethics would then be almost inevitable. Politics come to emphasise institutions with but scant mention of their ideals. This is borne out by contemporary European and American discussions on ethics and politics. On the one hand, it is suggested that to call something good is really to recommend it: that, rather than any possible intended naturalistic description, being held to be the point of calling it good. On the other hand, it is also suggested that all ideals which are realisable have certain specific institutions geared on to them in a proprietary manner. The question of the practicability of the ideals is then identified with the question of the acceptability and efficacy

47

of the named institutions. Identifying those two questions leads to much controversy, for the propriety of such a step is indeed questionable. In a sense, even, the disputes in religion, literature, philosophy are finally the same, corresponding in their basic features to the distinction between nature and super-nature. Philosophy can be seen as the secularisation of such a distinction. That is, in philosophy, the distinction is discussed without reference to that antenna of recommendation which ideals hang out. The distinction is made cold, even brutal. In philosophy, the dispute reaches its critical point when art is identified with reality, supernature with nature itself, ideals with mere truths, fiction with history. And this interlocking is generalised in that account which alleges that what is said to be objective is nothing but the reconciliation or coincidence of many subjective views, or in that account of reality which treats it as the way things appear in normal and standard conditions. Here appearance and reality incontinently interlock. Reality becomes appearance, so to say, in Sunday clothes. History becomes a kind of fiction in so far as creative imagination is given play in it. This is Trevor-Roper's recommendation. Fiction in comparative mythology is treated as being in its essence history. Ideals become truths to which attention needs to be drawn, and those who do not share the ideals are called perverse or blind. Art becomes a deep reality, the artist a kind of scientist using different apparatuses, and speaking different languages. Ideals, fiction, art, all come to be said to be true; and so do truths, history, science. Morality, what the people want or say, instead of making out the voice of the people to be the voice of God by a sort of oxymoron makes out the voice of God to be the voice of the people. And God becomes one of us again. All this is only a by-product of the rise of science and technology.

Though the world was metaphysical to the Akan mind, not all problems admitted of metaphysical solutions. Hence, it is wrong to infer that the Akan had neither science nor technology. Nor, however, is this a greedy attempt to have it both ways. The Akan had iron and steel enterprises. Iron and steel implements have been discovered; and the sites of some foundries have also been unearthed. They had brassware, some of which seems however to have been imported. They had precious metal ornaments and their artistry and skill in the treatment of gold and jewellery impressed the early European visitors. With the possible exception of preventive medicine, medicine too was not for them a question of the analysis of concepts. The operation of metaphysics here was not in prognosis, diagnosis, or prescription. These questions were settled through naturalistic means. And herbal treatment was developed to a high degree of efficacy. To this day, this is the form of treatment to which by far the larger part of the population has reasonably easy access. When, however, questions of prognosis, diagnosis, and prescription had been solved, there was recognised a residual question, the question of that particular conjunction of circumstances, which, in the particular case of the patient, constituted his disease. The way in which this became a question was evidently through its being regarded as unique, that is, through the thought that the individual affected is a constant, not a variable in the disease situation. When the individual, as well as the conjoining circumstances, is regarded as a variable and not a constant in the disease situation, experiments become *theoretically* justified, the individual case acquires not a holy interest but a scientific curiosity-value, and the stage is set for a naturalistic theory of disease. In such a case, sacrifices, by way of thanksgiving, will not be any longer called for. Though an avoidance of the conjunction of circumstances which constituted the disease situation was traditionally recommended by the Akans, and though sanitary measures, both private and public, and also regulated feeding and drinking had always been counsels of prudence, the uniqueness of the patient, which the metaphysical view postulated, created in them a sense of the possibility of divine intervention. Hence it was to human interest that sacrifices and prayers should be offered for regained or continued good health.

One aspect of this view is the limitation which is involved on the operation of the concept of accidents. The occurrence of accidents was not itself denied. The world admits of accidents both as a scientific corpus and as a metaphysical corpus.

49

Accidents in a scientific corpus include conjunctions for which no law is known; in the metaphysical corpus, they include conjunctions the concepts of whose elements are held to be irrelevant to each other. And though relevance in the one view can be established through empirical (even statistical) evidence, in the other view it is exclusively through the analysis of concepts.

Gods, in such a view as the Akans had, were not an invention of priests and priestesses. It is grossly wrong to think that here nature is spiritualised. Nature was in fact relatively insignificant. To state the metaphysical view in terms of a spiritualising of nature is to falsify the view altogether. It is to try to state it in terms of a position with which it is in radical conflict, for in the Akan view, nature was, if you like, supernature, antecedently spiritual.

In the Akan metaphysic, what is is in the first place spirit. Spirits exist in a hierarchy because the primary properties of spirits are qualities, those which are called moral: intelligence, courage, virtues, *et cetera*. There is of course a distinction between properties and qualities, properties being neutral and germane to descriptions, while qualities are tendentious, and germane to appraisals. Properties may be said to be naturalistic, and qualities to be moral. This distinction, however, is naturally a distinction of analysis, not of being, for the same aspects of an object may be properties now, and now qualities. The existence of a purpose, for example, is often sufficient to turn properties into qualities; thus, the properties of steel may be its qualities for some specific purpose. The purpose makes properties subject to suitability appraisals, and so makes them qualities. This distinction is possible only in a language in which the sense of the naturalistic is quite strong. In a metaphysical view, the feasibility of the distinction varies inversely with the dominance of metaphysics. In any case, there are in this view, qualities which have not become qualities; that is, qualities which are qualities, not in relation to some specific purpose or variable end, but are, in a way of speaking, qualities in their own proper being, either as ends in themselves, or as eminently suitable to fixed and unchanging ends. In brief then, any property could become a quality, but some qualities have never been properties. One point which emerges from this is that in the Akan metaphysics, certain entities have qualities for their properties and this immediately introduces a hierarchy of beings, and also determines the positions of objects in this hierarchy according as they have qualities or properties. Nonliving things belong to the lower ends of the hierarchy. Objects associated with spirits, including the human body, belong to the middle portions. And spirits, including that spirit which is proper to man, belong to the upper reaches. The whole forms one internally contiguous order. The contiguity of the order in which living beings are placed in a hierarchy immediately poses problems for religion. And to this attention may now be turned.

Its Supernatural Aspect

The Akan State was a sacred state in the sense that it was conceived as falling inside a world inhabited by human beings as well as spirits and gods, to whom human beings owed specific duties discharged through appropriate rites, and with whom human beings were in constant communion on the grounds of kinship. Spiritual kinship was the central form of kinship among the Akans and can even be used to explain their matrilinearity. A human being was for them an incapsulated spirit, and not an animated body as the Genesis story has it. The obligations of spiritual kinship took precedence over those of biological kinship, and the matrilineal descent is an expression of this hierarchy of kinship with its obligations. In what way it expresses it will become clear when the Akan family is discussed.

Living men too were essentially spirit, even if encased in flesh for a time. This has consequences for religion. Either the State itself is said to be religious because composed in the main of spirit, or the worshipful attitude of men becomes limited because they are themselves spiritual. It is when man is regarded as a substantive species in himself that the worshipful attitude has its best chance of occurrence. When man is regarded as partaking of the nature of the object of worship, then the actual degree of his worship must be lower than if he were not. Indeed, if a distinction can be drawn between worship and serving, then the Akans never had a word for worship. Worship is a concept that had no place in Akan thought. It was more completely absent among the Akans than among even the ancient Greeks who worshipped standing, on the grounds that only slaves bent their backs. Furthermore, the Akan theory of destiny even more thoroughly than their theory of the essence of man hampered worship. Each man was a spirit sent into the visible and natural world to fulfil a particular mission. This was not a point of view attained through reflection on human inequalities, though indeed one might argue that human inequalities become so startling that they are suggestive of fatalism. Rather, the Akan view of destiny was simply consonant with their idea of the perfectly integrated and co-hesive society in which men have a place somewhat comparable to the parts of a machine. Their place is appointed in it, and in that place they function for the total harmony and well-being. With the Akans it is nearer the truth to describe the State itself as being religious. The Akans did not conceive the world in terms of the supposition of an unbridgeable distance between two worlds, the temporal and the non-temporal, in terms of the supposition that of the two the latter was infinitely the better and the more important; in terms of that idea of some presence outside religious practitioners at which they aim, and which gives rise to a certain type of feeling including the feeling of reverence and self-abasement, characteristics in-gredient in the worshipful attitude. Because we were all religious objects, there was not sufficient externality and profundity to call for worship and religion in that sense. As men, that is to say, as accidents, we owed our existence to God; as spirits, that is to say, in our essence, we were uncreated. For this reason, even as men, we were said to be not God's creatures, but his messengers.

God himself was well to the fore of Akan thinking. He luxuriated in various by-names, of which *Onyame* seems to be central. Quite a few writers, Westerman, Rattray, and latterly Meyerowitz among them, have sought to identify *Onyame* or

Nyame as a sky-god, because of a supposed etymology. It is thought by them that *Nyame* is derived from *nyam* or *onyam*. There is indeed a verb *nyam* in Akan, usually used of witches. In this use, it refers to their rapid and phosphorescent movements this way and that when performing. But this can hardly be the derivation of the name of the Supreme Being. Also, there is a noun, and a cognate adjective, *onyam* meaning dignity, majesty, glory. These are all epithet nouns which admittedly are applied in Akan theology to God. But it is arbitrary to insist that they have an origin in the sun. The Christian or Moslem God is no more a sky-god than the Akan, because the same epithets apply. The identification of the Akan God with a sky-god is encouraged by the lexicographer Chrystaller's rendering of *Onyame* in his great Akan-English dictionary. Here he *conjectures* that *onyame* is the Akan word for heaven, sky. He invokes a comparison between *nyam* and the root *dio* in Sanscritic languages. Here, he suffers himself to be misled by Sanscritic languages which he assumes, without offering any reason, to be similar to the otherwise disparate Akan in the derivations of the name of God. What he does is, therefore, in effect to have a name for God's abode but no name for God, for Chrystaller himself allows the other bynames of God to be of *subsequent* origin to *onyame*. Now, the word *onyame* does not itself mean sky, heaven, at all, but is only used by metonymy to refer to heaven, just as 'heaven' is sometimes used to refer to, but does not mean, God. In Chrystaller's own translation of the Bible into Akan, not once is *onyame* used for the heavens. He always uses the proper Akan word for it: *osor*. In his dictionary, he gives the correct Akan word for sky: *ewim* (ie the regions of the sun).

I do not, in fact, believe that *onyame* means the shining one either. If it meant the shining one, this would be the sun. At least God would then have to be associated with temporal epiphanies or associated—what is more far-fetched—with a shining domicile. Neither of these hypotheses is in fact fulfilled among the Akans; for on the one hand *Onyame* is thought to be invisible and not to have any epiphanies (it is indeed for this reason that he has no images or shrines). On the other hand he

53

is not held to live in the sky by name, but simply above, up there. An Akan myth about the location of heaven seems to connect it, though not to identify it, with the sky. The sky is conceived as an object, a sort of ceiling to the world, perhaps, even, the floor of heaven. According to this myth, once upon a time, when our ancestors were young, God lived very close to us. One day, however, a certain old woman, who was pounding her *fufu* (a plantain meal) with pestle and mortar, struck heaven with her pestle. Whereupon God said to her: 'Why do you do this to me? Because of what you have done, I am taking myself far up.' And, true to his word, as was to be expected, God betook himself far up. The myth goes on to present a sort of Tower of Babel story with a more tragic ending. The old woman, regretting that God was no longer near to man, asked all her children to gather together all the mortars they could find, and by building them one upon another, reach up to God on high. The children were dutiful enough, but found that they were one mortar short. The old woman, evidently quite senile by now, having taken thought, spoke again thus: 'Children, remove the bottom-most mortar, and by placing it on the top one so reach God at last.' Once more the dutiful children did as they were bidden. But now all the mortars collapsed, rolled to the ground, and all the children perished. A remarkable story, but it does not identify God's dwelling-place with the sky, though it connects them.

If *Onyame* is the central name of God, then it must express a strikingly theological meaning. And, from the proliferation of minor deities which the Akans claimed to be an avenue to God's munificence and bountiful protection, I am led to believe that the correct and proper derivation of *Onyame* or *Nyame* is *nya:* to get or *onya:* fortunate possession and *mee:* be satisfied, want nothing. This derivation would appear to be confirmed by the assiduity and frequency with which the Akans appealed for all sorts of help to minor deities whom they conceived as lieutenants of the Supreme Being, almost even as the expression of his omnipotence.

Some writers who have been struck by the Akan conception of the Supreme Being as the one true God have claimed, mistakenly, that he was imported from Europe. But the per-spicuous Rattray has already refuted this opinion. Onyame is too central to the speech and thought of the Akans, he figures in the immemorial prologue to Akan ceremonial drumming, and he was well-known in the deepest fastnesses of the forest where missionary zeal had not been. If he were of European import, the amount of diffusion which would have to be supposed to explain the thorough permeation of thought and speech by 'Onyame', would properly belong to the realm of fantasy. Indeed the Akans believe the knowledge of God to be intuitive and immediate. This is suggested by the adage: '*Obi nnkyere abofra Nyame.*' 'No-one teaches a child God.'

The properties of God were signalised in his other by-names, chief of which was *Onyankopon* or *Nyankopon*. This is usually said to mean one-who-bears-the-weight-of-others-without-crooking. The idea is that the word is derived from *nya:* one, he; *nko:* alone; *mmpon:* crook not, bend not. But Rattray re-ports that the word among the Akims, a sub-group of the Akans, was in his time *Onyame-nko-pon*, which means the alone great God. There is also a third account which is somewhat bizarre, according to which the proper derivation is from *onyan:* brightness; *koro:* city; *pon:* great, the great sky city. The method of teaching, that of oral instruction, would seem to make the occurrence of *Onyame-nko-pon* significant. It suggests this as the original form from which *Onyankopon* was contracted. In that case, the intended meaning of the latter would be the meaning of the former. Some confirmation may be seen for this in the occurrence of another by-name of God, *Twereduampon*, or, among the Fantis, a coastal sub-group of the Akans, *Twereampon*. The suggested derivation is *twere:* lean on; *dua:* tree; *ammpon:* bend not. Hence the idea of God as that on whom one leans with safety is already explicit in this by-name. Here again the more explicit form would be the older one. Now if in this by-name of God he is explicitly said to be dependable for leaning on, then in view of the rival etymologies suggested for *Nyankopon*, it would not be reasonable to hold it too as expressing the same dependability. I myself am drawn to the meaning, the alone great God. He is also called *Otumfuo* (the mightiest and most powerful by right and fact); *Odomankoma* (Prometheus, Inventor); *Onyankopon Kwame* (Onyankopon, whose day is Saturday); *Borebore* (maker of things). God is invisible, but is everywhere, and is directly accessible. The Akans say that if you wish to say something to God, tell it to the wind.

It has often been said by European writers on the Akan that Nyame has no interest in morality. This remark can only have arisen out of ignorance. Onyame is conceived by the Akans to be so interested in justice that he gave two different names to two different things that there might not be injustice. He is full of love, and is even said to pound *fufu* for the cripple. This compares with the saying that God cares for the tailless animal. He is, however, at the same time unchangeable, though subject to his own laws. He is the appointer of destiny, and there is a saying that there are no sidepaths from the destiny which God appoints. Finally, to sum up the attitude to God, one might quote the Akan saying according to which the earth is vast, but God is the chief. He is said to be always creating.

The proliferation of gods that one finds among the Akans is in fact among the Akans themselves superstitious. Minor gods are artificial means to the bounty of Onyame. They are instituted by priests between man and God, with the explanation that they are portions of God's virtue and power sent to men for their speedy comfort through the exclusive intervention of the priests who also are their guardians. If one thinks of saints and priests in Christianity, one is enabled to form a quick idea of the artificiality of minor deities among the Akans. Intercession through the saints is comparable in intention to intercession through the minor deities. This comparison has in fact been made by Arthur Ramos and Bastide in discussing syncretism in South America. The Christian God has no feast-day, except, doubtfully, the Sunday of Holy Trinity. Similarly, Onyame has no feast-day. Feast-days belong to the minor deities. In ritual, the gods are in fact enslaved, for when the correct rite has been performed, the recipient of the rite is left little choice. Ritual is a quasi-magical set of exercises. The institution of minor deities thus appears as an attempt to make sure of God's succour and even influence it. For this reason, there are no rites for Nyame, and it would be impious to set oneself up as his priest, the man who has a private extension to him, and who knows his special magical rites. For the same reason, Nyame has no altar. To address him, you speak to the wind.

The priest, by claiming special connections with minor deities and hence indirectly with God, was enabled to become oracular. In this way, his influence spread from the religious to the purely social. Omniscience is not a widespread property of man, and the priest became consulted as a supposedly unfailing source of information. People came to appeal to him as one might appeal to the Encyclopaedia or the Criminal Investigation Department. The Criminal Investigation Department is a profane organisation, and its profanity consists in the declared method of operation. The sacredness of the priest too consisted in his declared method of operation, a hand-dip into the omniscience of *Odumankoma*, God. The real method of operation of the priest was, however, as profane, if not as fruitful, as that of the Criminal Investigation Department. He organised scouts who made enquiries and collected pieces of gossip and practically maintained extensive dossiers.

The minor deities were always associated with a focus to which they could be summoned at will. They are said by the priests to be sent by God himself, usually in a blinding flash of lightning. The priest, if he is alert enough, catches this piece of God's omnipotence, and imprisons it in a gourd—until he can prepare a proper focus for it, usually fashioned out of stone or wood, which is acceptable to it. After this, it becomes an intermediary between man and God. This focus is not in itself sacred, but becomes so only during those periods in which the minor deity enters it, whether summoned or not. The priest, of course, claims to be able to summon it to its focus, and the deity indicates his arrival through the priest's body being thrown into a fit of trembling. The priest is frequently a woman, and training before ordination takes two to three years.

That this was a superstitious corruption of the relation between man and God is evident enough from the theology of God. The priest as a mouthpiece of God (*Onyankupon Kyeame*) is an arrant blasphemy. To make this clear, one may consider that there is an Akan saying that no man's path lies in another's. This saying is linked with Akan views on destiny. It is believed that there is an aspect of man called *Okra* (literally, mission) which represents the destiny that God has appointed for him. Each man's spirit gives an account to Nyame at death, and might be allowed to come into the world of flesh again, or he might be detained at Samanadze where the spirits of the dead wander. That the relation between each man and God is direct and exclusive is further suggested by the sayings that when one's spirit takes leave of God to become a man, there are no witnesses; nor are there sidepaths to the destiny that God has appointed for one; a sensible man does not try to change the words that God has spoken beforehand; if God has not fixed one's death, and a human being tries to kill one, one does not die; and if God fills one's cup with wine and a mortal stumbles over it, God fills it up for one again. These sayings fully suggest the fatality and loneliness of life. And the resort to priests and their minor deities appears as an attempt to derive some comfort in face of this fatality and loneliness of life. This spiritual atomism is in direct contrast with the social organisation of the Akan. The latter will be taken up in its place.

God was mainly put to two kinds of use. Supplications could naturally be addressed to him directly, and the satisfaction which he gave was thought to be complete. Each household had a *Nyame Dua*, which was a forked post. On the fork was fitted a pot or bowl containing a stone axe-head, never used as an axe but believed to be planted in the earth by lightning. In the pot was also some water containing specific herbs. The courtyard and even the people were sprinkled with the water in the morning as a prayer for God's continued protection. The *Nyame Dua* is a sign of acknowledgement of our dependence on God. Along with the idea of destiny, God was also used to explain striking talents and special aptitudes. Thus, there is a saying that one does not teach the son of the smith how to forge, God does. And again, if God did not give the remarkable swallow anything, at least he endowed it with swiftness in turning. The occasions on which God is invoked are many and diverse,

But in particular he is invoked at the installation of chiefs and in the official drummer's preface.

Its Theory of Man and Society

One may wish to pose two questions here: first, whether general procedures of psychology are applicable in Africa, and, second, whether findings by psychologists who have studied European communities might stand in Africa without being further checked; or might the psyche of Africans turn out to be quite distinct and not really support the findings of European psychologists who have studied Europe? One may of course wish to pose a third question, the question whether Africans have theories of the resolution of their own psyche. The way in which a people resolve their psyche into aspects is bound to affect the explanations which they give of human behaviour. And the two together affect the way in which their society is set up and run. Freud, for example, is largely responsible for the ever-growing tendency to treat certain evil-doers as sick men, through his account of the human psyche.

The Akans were not without such an account. In a human being, apart from his body, the Akans distinguished the *okra*. The *okra* is the guiding spirit of a man, the bearer and instrument of his destiny, that in a man which antecedently to the incarnation takes its leave of God. The *okra* is also that whose departure from the living man means death, and marks the completion of his destiny. It returns to God to justify its earthly existence. So important is this held to be that there is an Akan saying to the effect that all men are children of God, and no man is a child of the earth. Only human beings have an *okra*. The *okra* is capable of appearing time after time on earth in different bodies, and it is the crucial factor in personal identity. This is what encourages the Akans to talk of a person's real self.

The *okra*, by being the bearer of destiny, lends its name to signal good luck and signal bad luck, both being thought in a way to be deserved, or at least unavoidable and perhaps even fitting. When either takes place, one says it is the person's *okra*. It is believed that the *okra* of a person can be interrogated by priests while it is still in the mother's womb. This, again, is an impious attempt to scrutinise and perhaps divert what God has laid down beforehand. In Akan mysticism, it must consequently be adjudged to be superstitious.

In addition to the *okra*, the Akans distinguished the *Sunsum* of a man. The *okra* was conceived to be automatic in its functioning, even when it gives advice which is good or bad. Its advice does not arise from any interest, but from the ineluctable unfolding of the destiny appointed for it. In face of danger it can therefore be the means of its possessor's salvation to prevent death betimes. The saying that someone dies betimes is consequently, to speak strictly, quite meaningless in Akan conceptualism.

The destiny of a man was called his *nkrabea*. His *nkrabea* often appeared as an encumbrance to him, for though the *okra* was the basis of his personal identity, the living man did not identify himself with his *okra*, and of a man whose *okra* did not, so to say, bring him good luck, it was said that he had *okrabiri* (a black *okra*). It was said that a man whose *okra* was pink always ate berries and tender fruits and wore embroidered linen. By contrast, if a man's *okra* was black, that was an abomination; application brought him no gain. Trouble searched him out.

Sunsum appears to have been a spiritual substance responsible for *suban*, character, genius, temper and quality. *Sunsum* is moral in its operation, not automatic, and is educable. Whereas the *kra* is that which makes a person breathe and so is the principle of life, the *sunsum* is not, and is thought to be able to leave a man during sleep. It is that second man who is a *dramatis persona* in dreams. A man's *sunsum* is also that spirit of a man which may be attacked by witchcraft. The *sunsum* as the basis of character is said to be strong or wicked or good. And when a person is a witch or wizard, it is through the power of the *sunsum*.

The Akans also distinguished the *ntoro*. The *ntoro* is inheritable, but not the *sunsum* or the *okra*. The *ntoro* does not at death depart with the *okra*, but goes down to a man's children or, failing these, to his nephews and nieces by his brother. The father's *ntoro* takes the place of the child's *ntoro* until the child attains puberty. Puberty among the Akans is not tied to any particular age, but is claimed with the appearance and luxuriance of pubic hairs. The child's own *sunsum* begins to operate at puberty. But its father's *ntoro* does not for this reason cease altogether to be operative. The *ntoro* of the father is cited by the Akans in explanation of inherited characteristics, and is also thought of as a group of characteristics, a type of personality. And it is the co-operation of the father's *ntoro* with the mother's blood in the sense of kinship which is believed to form the foetus and mould it into the form of a human being.

Finally, the Akans distinguished the *mogya* which is a type of spiritual factor, and is the basis of the *abusua* or clan. This can only be bestowed by females. It is the *mogya* which at the death of a person becomes his *saman* (ghost). As a *saman* it retains the bodily form. It has a chance of reincarnation though this is only possible through a woman of the same clan. Not even reincarnation can make a person change clan.

From the Akan theory of man it is evident that human personality and character were seen by them to rest on a number of factors and influences; comprising the *okra*, which above all was the ineducable and unswervable element; the *sunsum*, which was educable through precept and a system of punishment and reward, and was the foundation of personal and moral responsibility; the *ntoro* which was inherited and related mainly to the prescription of certain practices and the avoidance of others, thereby moulding temperament through the operation of taboos; and finally the *mogya* which ensured that one was amenable to reason, made one a human being. In the Akan theory of man, consequently, spiritual factors were primary.

A man was thought to be survived at death by his *okra* which went back to *Nyankopon*, and by his *mogya* which became his *saman*, and bore a physical resemblance to him. It is this *mogya* as *saman* which is invoked in what is miscalled ancestor worship.

Three kinds of *nsamanfo* were distinguished. There was the *samanpa* or good *saman*. A *saman* was deemed good if the death of the man was not followed either by a run of general bad luck, including further deaths, for his family or even community, or if his death was followed by the cessation of a previous run of bad luck. These ghosts are shy, and hide round corners when they see a man.

There was the *saman-twen-twen*, the ghost which could not be laid. Such a ghost was seen at intervals by living persons around the man's old haunts. They were incapable of going to the spirit world where their like are. They hung around dark corners and back-yards. They hung around the earth as a temporary or everlasting punishment. They had not much power for harm and contented themselves with scarifications.

Finally, there was also the *tofo*, the ghost of a man who met a violent death. As being unlucky, such a man was given specially deprecatory burial rites. These ghosts cannot get on with the good ones; they wander about, painted with white clay, and clothed in white raiment. But unlike the good ones, they are bold and aggressive.

Ghosts were associated with a particular odour said to be like that of *nunum*, a certain aromatic plant. A ghost is, when visible, always dressed in white. It is not an object of friendship; and you are cautioned that if one should offer you its hand, you quickly bend yours away. A good ghost, however, showers blessings on its orphan. Ghosts have analogues of human senses and passions, including those of hunger, thirst, and anger. Quite impolitely, they sometimes invite themselves to meals, a sure sign of their activity being the too-rapid disappearance of food and drink with which everyone is familiar. To forestall this people often drop a morsel on the ground to distract ghosts. Stools are often tilted when not in use to prevent stray and tired ghosts from sitting on them; and should a person sit on one before a ghost can get away, he contracts pains in the waist.

Ghosts by and large inhabit the spirit world. There is a half-cynical, half-reverent attitude to this world illustrated in the saying that if the spirit world has nothing to it, at least it has its name behind it. Each man has to go there himself, messages are neither sent nor carried. Nor does one go there oneself and return as one pleases. If Orpheus had been an Akan, he would not have known any route save death to the underworld. The spirit world has a social organisation complete with chiefs and subjects. But opinion is not certain about its location.

Some say it is under the earth. Some say it is up in the skies. But there is always a route to it from one's grave wherever one is buried. It is an extensive country and the journey there takes one over mountains. The track to the spirit world of a man who dies a peaceful death is dark and unluminous. But a man who dies a violent death drops some of the white clay off him on his track, and this is why the milky way is white. At the same time there is a compresence between spirits and men. And the chief difficulty of going to the spirit world is not navigational, but one of transformation. Since heaven is in a sense around us, to speak to God one speaks to the wind. In the same way the spirits of our ancestors are always within call, and can be summoned at will through ritual invocation without raising the voice.

In what is called ancestor-worship, ancestors are invoked to give succour to their family descendants. A great deal of respect is shown to them on such occasions. The basis of the respect is twofold, first that the ancestors are our predecessors, our elders, and for this reason alone command our respect; and second that in their spiritual state they note more than we can, being in unhindered touch with the essence of things. The ceremony of ancestor-worship is also an occasion for remembering them, a sort of family reunion. An Akan family can only grow, it cannot diminish, for the ancestors are continuing members of it. But because they no longer belong to the three-dimensional order of things, specialised avenues of consultation have to be devised to reach them. This creates the need for rites. The rites of ancestor-worship are not rites of worship but methods of communication. There is no feeling of self-abasement and self-negation on the part of the living during such rites. The lineages to which the ancestors belong are not political devices, though they lend themselves to use in sorting out political claims. In themselves they are antecedent to political arrangements, and this indeed is the reason why they can be cited in evidence of political claims. The permanence of the lineage is also a method of family archive.

The lineage is an extremely formal sequence, complete with its totem, its taboos, and even its personality. Personality implies a high degree of integration and systematisation. The clue to this is to be found in statements to the effect that such and such a thing is not in character. A nation has no personality unless it is highly systematised in its attitudes and in its responses. A lineage, because it is for these purposes a closed system, has a personality which may in fact be called its group personality. The notion of a group personality is not a far-fetched one and may be referred readily to heaven and hell because of the systematisation involved in the conception of these. In any case, the inheritability of the *ntoro* and the *mogya* gives additional unity to the lineage traced matrilineally, and reinforces the group personality. The inter-relation of the several lineages in the community in a definite way bestows a certain formality on the larger society too, and creates the foundation of the community personality. This community personality is the crux of the Akan theory of the State. The State is almost personified, and takes precedence over every individual. So does the *Abusua* or clan. Between the *Abusua* and the *Oman* (State), the *Oman* is supreme. The kinship involved in the *Abusua* organisation first and foremost places duties on its members. This is how the Akan society comes to be founded on duties rather than rights. The duties are both ritualistic and humanist. The ritualistic duties consolidate the clan at the spiritual level. The humanistic ones consolidate it at the human level. The responsibility of a member of the clan for the welfare of other members is nevertheless not calculated to encourage the lazy and indolent. It has no suggestion of anyone rushing out of step to save the needy but foolish. There are a great many sayings all tending to this point. When you are needy, you do pick nuts from a dung heap, runs one. This does little towards conjuring a picture of clansmen thrusting their bounty on one. A few more run as follows:

When you are needy, you eat the skin of a goat;
Need turns a nobleman into a slave;
Poverty is like madness (in what it makes you do).

The responsibility of your clansmen takes effect when you are a stranger in a village, or when without your fault you become indigent or fall into debt, and are quite close to the last ditch. To confirm this need for solidarity and permanence, there is a saying that a clan is like a flowering shrub, it blossoms in clusters. There is another saying that the family tree is not clipped.

Though clans were basic to the State, they were not co-ordinate in importance. There was a clan or a hierarchy of clans from which alone rulers could be elected, other things being equal. The Akans say that all clans are equally clans and good enough at that; but we nevertheless look closely at the nuts of the oil-palm. The establishment of a hierarchy among clans was evidently a cohesive device for the *Oman*, for it created the basis of leadership, and the authority for command, and thereby lessened power-struggle of a disintegrative kind, while at the same time preserving a democracy of leadership through elections.

The whole education of youth was given a utilitarian orienta-tion. The *Oman* included venerable ancestors, and in a way reflected in visible embodiment the structure of the spiritual world with which it was in continuous touch. It was therefore in effect a religious set-up. It was to the nurture of this religious set-up that the education of youth was directed. An admonitory saying holds that when the State begins to collapse, the cause can be found in the home. Another, which emphasises the completeness of the individual's absorption in the *Oman*, held that if the State or the people cut silly patterns on the hair of one's head, one did not erase them. The absoluteness of the State's claim on the individual's obedience was in this saying endorsed. The State's call on the individual was, however, not arbitrary and gratuitous but based on reflection and decision of a public kind, and tending towards the public good.

The opinion is often expressed that the coherence of tradi-tional African societies set close limits on individual freedom and initiative, and might even be expected to have produced a great deal of pusillanimity. There possibly is a misconception here. In any State, instruments must be devised for preserving public peace and establishing a range of public harmony and efficiency. In modern States, there are legal organisations to

65

preserve peace, and clusters of professional and semi-professional organisations to lay down additional rules of conduct, e.g. for the press, for lawyers, for doctors, tennis players, *et cetera;* there are clubs and also public opinion to establish a range of harmony through ideas about things which are not done, and things which one may do. In a society which is not organised in these ways, the purposes which these bodies serve are still legitimate and desirable. The intense development of the communal spirit becomes an optimum way of securing these ends. The communal spirit was in fact raised in Akan society through education and public opinion. When the bodies and clubs referred to come into existence, individuals are freed from their pertinent *direct* obligations to the community, and express these obligations *indirectly* through allegiance to these bodies and clubs. The obligations are still there; what has altered is their visibility. But because these obligations become more narrowly centred now, the individual obtains a sense of liberation, initiative and creativeness. The division of the Akan state into clans was in fact also a way of lightening the weight of the State on the back of the individual. The individual could concentrate on nurturing the clan instead of feeling directly responsible for the world. The clan was an instrument of making the communal spirit effective.

Inevitably, this subservience to the clan, because it made one's obligations to it moral and spiritual, tended to limit one's freedom of expression and action more than a merely social loyalty to a club or professional loyalty to an organisation might do. The reprisals which disloyalty involved were, not unexpectedly, quite grave. Disloyalty in the communalistic set-up was held to endanger the very fabric of society extending to and including the spirits of departed ancestors. Disloyalty to the clan could therefore in certain cases carry the aura of sacrilege. Disloyalty to a club or a professional organisation, because more limited in direction, often carries with it nothing more serious than expulsion or the demand for an apology. Here society is not enabled to feel immediately threatened as disloyalty to the clan led it to feel.

But if the clan limited the freedom of expression and action, and even the variety of feeling of its members, it is not to be inferred that thought was thwarted and stifled. The embargo on the expression of certain dangerous and impious opinions operated only in the presence of one's elders. School-teachers have in fact complained about the difficulty of getting African children to express definite opinions in speech. The cause of this is not any lack of definite, vigorous, original and creative thoughts, but the inability through upbringing to join issue with one's elders, in this case teachers. The essays written by the same children do not square with their public speech. This habit extends from primary schools to universities. There is an Akan saying that the words of one's elders are greater than an amulet. Elders were the repository of communal wisdom, and were not to be gainsaid lightly. The justification for this attitude lay in the fact that the wisdom of Africa was practical. In theoretical matters, where errors might have no more radical consequences than the waste of time and effort, dispute between learners and people who know better may be inconsequential, and even a healthy exercise. Where elders occupy a hierarchic position, public disputes with younger and lower persons cannot but bring a loss of dignity and effectiveness to their position. The wisdom which they represented might have been adequate to clan needs and state needs in their time. They are not adequate today. And in the age of searchings and seekings, disputes with them have become thinkable.

The restriction on action was largely limited to the choice of a wife and the choice of a career. In marriage, ideas about clan descent became operative. Akan clans are exogamous, exception being made only for kings, for a certain reason. The reason for the exception was interestingly identical with the reason for the general rule. As to the limitation on the freedom to choose a career, this could be expected in any society which had no notable surpluses of goods and wealth. The Akan society had a subsistence economy with very little surplus. The opportunities in such a society would be few, as they were in Akan society, and pure scholars had to depend exclusively on courtly patronage. Since the fortunes of an individual were connected with those of his families, his choice of a career was a matter integral to the family set-up. His fertility as a source of succour to the family in bad times, and his liability to claim succour from the family, made his choice of career susceptible to their feelings and opinions. Careers were chosen not as a means to self-fulfilment, but as a discharge of family responsibility. With the expansion of opportunities more members of a family can exert themselves both in their own favour and in that of their family. The larger the number of those who can do this, the less is their risk of being called upon to help, the greater therefore is their emancipation.

In art and literature and technology the canons of acceptability were dependent more on the individual apprehension than on social necessity.

The reason which explains the exogamy of the clan and the endogamy of the chief also explains the right of succession. The right of succession cannot be understood without the theory of ownership. The Akans recognised both private ownership and public ownership. In fact, their insight into the effects of private ownership was considerable. Land was the central object owned publicly. The land of a clan is jointly owned in perpetuity by the whole clan including the dead ancestors, and may not be alienated either in part or in whole. Freehold of land was unprovided for in the land tenure system. In England, there is no such thing as absolute ownership in the soil, the ultimate landowner being the Sovereign on behalf of the State. The strongest form of ownership open to Her Majesty's subjects is involved in fee-simple absolute in possession. For practical purposes, this is tantamount to absolute ownership in the land. Among the Akans, the practice is comparable to the theory in England. Land was vested in the throne or stool of the chief who held it in trust for the people. Even the chief had no absolute ownership in the land. Land was classified in two ways, administrative and stool. Stool land could be used personally by the reigning paramount chief for as long as he was chief. Consent of the chief was necessary to permit interference with such land. The administrative land of the stool was, on the other hand, merely land over which the stool had jurisdiction. This was the terrestrial area of his subjects. The Akan political system distinguished between population and territory in order to establish a polity. The administrative land, the territory of the State, was equitably distributed for farming and occupation under the surveyance of the chief's court. This arrangement is quite general in Africa and is only somewhat modified by historical events; for example, in Uganda variations in detail can be explained in terms of the feudalistic elements introduced by Galla invaders.

The rarity of private ownership makes the appointment of successors a formalistic matter. Precedence in inheritance is in the following order:

(1) The eldest brother by the same mother
(2) the eldest son of eldest sister
(3) grandson through female line
(4) another branch of the same family
(5) a slave.

Though succession was formalistic, the needs of trusteeship made consideration of expediency relevant. The successor, like his predecessor, only held property in trust, and if unfitted for this office could be bypassed without fuss. An heir required formal as well as aptitude qualifications. Even bodily blemish, not to speak of incompetence, could lead to the preference of the eldest son of the eldest sister over the eldest brother by the same mother. Slaves were occasionally preferred to living members of the same family. One regulative principle cited in succession disputes says in so many words that when mother's sons are not exhausted, nephews do not inherit.

There of course is a reason for this succession arrangement. The source of the family was held to be the woman. Hence members of the family and the clan were identified matrilineally. It was the woman who gave birth to the child; in a visible way, the child was more obviously the woman's than the man's; it was nurtured by the woman's blood and carried in the woman's womb. *Mogya*, that factor which determined the child's form, was contributed entirely by the mother. There is a saying that it is your mother's child who is your kin. Possessiveness over property would be an inducement to restrict succession to people tracing their *mogya* to a common source. In the case of the king or paramount chief, marriage within the same clan was allowed to preserve the royalty of the clan and the complete authenticity of the king.

The line of succession was not unconnected with the type of social organisation. When social organisation becomes completely substantive, a thing in itself, which does not consult antecedent metaphysics, the society is run on an intensely economic basis. And where the economic functions of the male become impressive to a certain degree, the succession becomes patrilineal. Where the same functions are discharged by a woman, there, whether the society has reference to antecedent metaphysics or not, the society is matrilineal. In the Akan society of traditional purity, economic obligations towards the child were mainly fulfilled by the mother. The filial attachment to the mother was in turn considered to be unseverable, and there is a saying that when one's mother hits hard times, one does not leave her to make somebody else one's mother.

The upbringing of the child was extremely pragmatic. Great store was always set by experience and wisdom among the Akans. Virtue was inculcated more through exercise than through precept. As one can expect, there are several sayings underlining this idea. A few are listed here:

'A child who is to be successful is not reared exclusively on a bed of down.'

'It is the knife-blade without a safety handle which frees itself from the hands of the child.'

'If a child pretends to be dead and plays possum, you pretend to bury him.'

'If a child does nine mischievous things, five of them always come back to him.'

'If a child insists on clutching live coals, by all means let him; when he gets burnt you won't have to encourage him to throw them away.'

The words of one's elders are greater than an amulet. In these few quotations one can already gather that the Akans believed in the discipline of children, and entirely endorsed the right of age to instruct youth. Wisdom was always preferred to authority, as the arrangements of inheritance themselves suggest. The Akans said that there was an old man before a lord was born. Though the Akans loved wisdom greatly, their attitude towards fools was not one of harshness, but one of ridicule and mild contempt. Wisdom was always practical, the fool being the man who was constantly at a loss, and not simply a theoretically inept person. I set out a few sayings touching upon the fool.

'The fool says: they mean my friend, not me.'

Here the shiftlessness of the fool, his utter inability to profit from anything not shoved into his mouth, is meant. A wise man, one supposes, profits from everything.

'When you quote a proverb to a fool, you also need to explain it.'

'It is only the fool who needs a proverb explained to him.'

This is equivalent to the saying *verbum sapienti*.
Touching the improvidence of the fool, the Akans say that

'When he is squandering his gold, he says his scales are out of order.'

And since he does not do things with his eyes wide open, they say that

'It is the fool whose own tomatoes are sold to him.'

The Akans expressed their dislike for purely academic points in the saying that

'Wisdom is not like money to be tied up and hidden.'

The admonition to the wise to profit from every situation lends itself to a literal interpretation. In readiness for this possibility, the Akans wryly remark that

'When two astute persons deal with each other, feelings run high.'

In the same style of interpretation, it is said that

> 'The wise man levers eight pounds from a fool with the aid of a penny.'

This kind of dealing was not much praised and you are warned that

> 'Where you cheat the fool, a wise man sits and watches.'

The pragmatic and whimsical colour of Akan wisdom, which in fact pervades African wisdom in general, makes it immediately available for the modernistic reconstruction of African societies. The need for reconstruction is itself mainly pragmatic. Its problems will form the subject-matter of the last chapter. I shall content myself here with saying that the Akan attitudes as they affected life were in fact modernistic and mature. The communal spirit is strong at a certain low level of economic development, and its essentially negative character promises not to interfere with economic development. The preparation for the economic uplift of Africa will involve considerable pain and sacrifice which calls for the examination of African attitudes towards poverty and riches. Once again, one must turn to sayings in order to discover the principles underlying these attitudes and also the judgments liable to be made in money economy situations. Accordingly, I am setting down a few relevant sayings:

> 'In the extremes of need, a human being will live in the forest (like an animal).'
> 'Indigence will make one search for nuts in a dung-heap.'
> 'Poverty turns a nobleman into a slave.'
> 'Poverty is madness.'

This group of quotations illustrates the shifts to which poverty is capable of driving one. The likening of poverty to madness shows considerable insight into that appearance of unaccountability which poverty produces in certain temperaments. The Akans did not however win the release of creative energies which poverty is again capable of provoking. In their recognition of the harshness and cruelty which accompany such energies they showed their essential humanity. They even said, 'If Europe knew no poverty, the white man would not leave his people to live in the black man's country.' This reveals that the spirit with which some of the Akans defended themselves against European attempts to settle or alienate their land was not always due to the metaphysical entanglements in which they involved land in their thinking. The appreciation of the relevance of economic wants and motives to the brutalities of colonialism was quickly made. The likeness of poverty to madness was explored in specific sayings about the dispositions of the poor man.

'Poverty has no friends.'

In a strongly communalistic society, this makes one either a god or a beast.

'The poor man has no anger.'

Not because he is not provoked. Poverty and strength of personality were thought to be ill bedfellows, and the degradation of poverty was completed in statements like the following:

'The apophthegms of the poor are not quoted.'
'A poor man's suit is summarily disposed of.'
'When the poor man wears a necklace of the soft silky gorow, it is said he is wearing a sheep's halter.'
' "I am in need, please do this for me," that is how some became slaves.'

In this last saying, the Akans showed their regard for personal independence, and this was undoubtedly connected with the negative and conditional responsibility that the clan had for looking after individual members. Akan communalism bore striking resemblances to the Social Welfare State.

Personal thrift was enjoined and the lack of it was coupled with idiocy, as in the saying about the fool and his scales. Poverty, the Akans said, does not announce a date.

The connection between authority, prestige, and wealth was also noticed and felt.

'No one bullies another with his poverty.'

73

'The rich man is the man of authority.'
'Money is sharper than the sword.'
'When wealth came and passed by, nothing came after.'
'Money is like a servant, if you abuse it, it runs away.'
'When a rich man gets drunk, you say he is indisposed.'
'The misdeeds of a rich man are always invisible.'
'Fame of being nobly born does not spread, it is the fame of riches which spreads.'
'One does not cook one's nobility and eat, it is wealth that counts.'

Poverty was not necessarily connected with slavery by the Akans, though in general it was connected with status. A slave could through efficiency and competence even establish a claim to succession, and certainly at times became very wealthy. There were three ways in which one could become a slave. There were those who voluntarily placed themselves under a master for protection and food and shelter, or even for payment. Second, there were those who were pledged or pawned by their relatives to liquidate debts or as security for a debt. Included in this group were those who were forcibly seized in surety for a debt in what was known as *panyarring*. There were, thirdly, those who became slaves from being children of slaves. They were usually made to carry loads and help in the cultivation of farms.

Slaves were considered to form part of households, even if they were the lowest members. And though they were said not to choose their own masters, they were not treated with cruelty or contempt, for as the Akan saying had it, all men were children of God and no-one was a child of the earth. To people who were given to treating slaves badly, the question was rhetorically put whether one would say the big and heavy drum was good for Kobuobi to carry if he were one's mother's child. Theoretically, slaves could regain their freedom on grounds of cruelty. At the same time, it was said that one did not acquire a slave in order to be affronted by him. The impertinence of certain slaves was recorded in the saying that when a slave had amassed some wealth, he assigned himself to the Nsona, a leading clan. Slaves were allowed to use property that they had acquired as they pleased, and occasionally they became wealthier than their masters, gathered a larger retinue, and even commanded free soldiers.

At the same time, the slave was legally without responsibility, and acts committed, whether or not in pursuance of his master's bidding, were regarded as his master's act. He was responsible for his slave's debts and for compensation for injury inflicted by him. A slave's obedience was to his immediate master and could not be transitively claimed by his master's master. The origins of slavery were traced by the Akans to the loss of independence by shiftless persons, who depended on others for their livelihood and security. Apologists of the slave trade, which was completely out of touch with slavery among the Akans, said slanderously that if the Akans had the right to sell their children, strangers had the right to buy them. As early as 1749, Roemer, the Danish historian who had for a long time been in the Gold Coast and Ashanti, wrote a book refuting this allegation. The allegation was founded on a misunderstanding of the Akan word *oba*. The European merchants understood the sentence '*Me dze me ba bi aba*' to mean 'I have brought a son with me' instead of 'I have brought a fellow with me', said when people offered someone for sale.

Its Theory of Government

According to the Akan political theory, the whole power of a ruler was derived from the people and held in trust for them. This was safeguarded in the provision for the removal of rulers, and the grounds for such removal. But though this was a theory which founded sovereignty in the people, it was not entirely negative in its intent, but placed the whole consensus and force of the people behind the actions of rulers. The decisions of the ruler were indeed even put sometimes in the mouth of the people. Thus, it was said that if the people cut silly patterns on the hair of someone's head, he still could not wipe them out. To go against the consensus of the people even in expression of opinion, let alone action, was a piece of rashness looked upon with scant favour. The time to express one's eccentricity was in the period of deliberation. To persist in one's individual

75

opinion, when this deviated from the public opinion deliberately arrived at and publicised, was a piece of malice. The unity principle was very strongly cherished. Such luxuries as minority reports were therefore foreign to the political arrangements of the Akans.

It would be hasty to see in this a curb on the freedom of speech of the individual. It must be allowed even in the most radical liberalism, if a distinction can be sustained between it and anarchy at all, that there must be a point where the exercise of the freedom of speech becomes an aggression on the freedom of one's audience not to be pestered. The Akans are revealed by their sayings as a very practical-minded people. The value of the freedom of expression lay for them in the possible aspect of the truth which it might reveal. But if action is to be taken at all, then there is a point where discussion must end. The cessation of discussion does not, of course, close the logical possibility of valid criticism. But since action has to be taken in its time, the appearance of unanimity must be preserved at the time of action. Action which reveals unsettled conviction and polar attitudes might be said to exchange for an uncertainty of being right, the certainty of being wrong. The persistent expression of divergent views when a decision had been reached, was seen by the Akans, not unreasonably, as disruptive and divisive, and so weakening. It was therefore proscribed. This kind of proscription, in emphasising collective responsibility, strengthened unity, for public decisions were equally binding on all, irrespective of positions and views antecedent to their arrival.

But in order that the proscription of dissenting voices after decisions had been taken, unanimity failing, should not constitute too grave an injustice for any parties, arrangements were made for all opinions and points of view to be heard and discussed. Decision was based on consensus, which after all is the nearest practical equivalent to unanimity. In smaller communities, all citizens were summoned to the market place to make politic discussions. In larger communities, this was practically impossible and the discussion was primarily held by elected and representative chiefs of different clans, who advised the paramount chief. It was an Akan maxim that there was no such thing as a bad king, only bad counsellors.

Two things were involved in this maxim. There was first the subjection to the constitution involved for the paramount chief. And there was, secondly, the involvement of the whole community in decisions either directly through their own persons, or indirectly through their chiefly representatives elected by them. The equivalence thus secured between consensus and unanimity made the effects of decisions ineluctable. Appropriately there was a saying that if the king wished to kill one, it was useless casting lots. To leave no uncertainty about his authority, it was said that if he brought one hardship, it was from the people. The king appears to have been a person in whose mouth decisions were put. His own acquiescence was theoretically unnecessary though he was expected to give moral leadership. He had no right to make peace or war on his own initiative, or enter into negotiations or treaties touching on the interests of his people, or even make laws.

Because of his constitutional position, the paramount chief continuously depended for his well-being on his own ability and the opinion of his people and counsellors, and the sacred attitude to the State eliminated the selfish tendencies of power-struggles among the latter. With the death of a king, the properties of the State reverted to trusteeship of the Queen Mother, and the new king had first to prove his abilities before acquiring a right to the governorship of the properties. In the case of Kofi Karikari, for example, the nineteenth King of Ashanti in Ghana, slight but sinewy, hospitable and gracious, the state wealth was withheld from him for five years.

Kingship was more a sacred office than a political one, and because the king was surrounded by counsellors whose offices were political, and was himself only a representation of the spiritual unity of the people, it was quite possible to remove him from office; the catalogue of the possible grounds of removal was already held in advance.

A king could be removed from office for a variety of blemishes. A king who constantly insisted on his own apprehension of things against the combined apprehension of his elected counsellors could be removed. It was said that the people could not drink water with such a person. An oppressive, arbitrary and injurious king could be removed. A king could be removed for corruption, or neglect of the affairs of state, or lack of dignity with women. He could even be removed for contumacy to his counsellors. Should he be incapacitated by disease he was removed from office.

Nevertheless he was not easily dislodged, for even though he was tried without his knowledge, his counsellors had first to consult another body and secure their agreement that there was a charge against the king. If this agreement could not be obtained, the matter had to be dropped immediately. If the agreement was obtained, a secret court was held where witnesses gave evidence and were examined. A report was then formally sent to the head of the royal clan, who was different from the king. Lesser chiefs and heads of clans were then summoned together, and it was only by their unanimous decision that the king could be removed. He was sometimes even fined for offences for which he might be removed. There was a saying that the awe of the king was made by the king's servants. His ears were likened to an openwork basket; its avenues were more than a thousand. He was said to be like the *Odum* tree, without a front and without a rear. Hence nothing could be done or plotted behind the king's back.

The political administration of the Akan state was carried out through ministerial chiefs. The chiefs were elected to cater for certain specialisms or even ministries. Different chiefs were responsible for recitation, ceremony, publicity, the stool, graves, music, administration of the capital, the royal household, the royal bodyguard, the military.

The chief of recitations was responsible for keeping the records of the nation. There were songs of praise about the exploits of past men, the battles they won, the peoples they conquered and their outstanding characteristics. He supervised persons who were specially trained in the preservation of such details, and had much exercise in their composition in literary form. Moral didactic pieces were also preserved and handed down from singer to singer. Purely literary items for social enjoyment emerged from generation to generation, and were embellished and modified to bring their topicality up to date. Literary output included stories, novelettes, tableaux, vignettes, plays, poems, epics. In this way a literary language which was not used in common speech was evolved and perfected. The occasion for reciting history and praise-songs was ceremonial and a great deal of these were recited on the talking drums in the presence of the reigning king. In this way, examples of the great deeds of his predecessors were put before him, and he was exhorted to comparable heights of heroism and success. The songs also settled the terms and protocol with which the king was to be associated. They made him a focus of loyalty to the state, and damaged revolutionary fervour. A sub-group of the singers restricted themselves to a continual definition of the status and the functions of the current king, who was constantly referred to by means of praise and status-names.

The history which these recitations included was considerably vetted, and it carefully eschewed all reference to different origins of sections of the people in order to make their assimilation, and so the unity of the people, permanent and complete. The punishment for indiscretions in this respect was death, and was immediate. An executioner was purposefully stationed behind such official historians. The Ashanti empire in particular grew by conquest and a sort of integrated accretion. Every effort was made to obliterate the seams, the true history and origins of the conquered peoples caught in the Ashanti vortex. Court historians of such peoples were brought to the Ashanti court at Kumasi where they were diligently re-educated in their new and official history. The Ashantis proudly likened themselves to the porcupine, peace-loving at normal, but not to be aroused with impunity, endowed with hosts of quills all united in a common purpose, and in a common centre. The king of Ashanti was by far the most resplendent and powerful of the Akan kings at any time.

The *Akyeamehene* was the chief of the king's spokesmen, for the king may not himself speak directly to his people. The chief of the stool-carriers, with his lieutenants, was responsible for carrying the chief's stool around and making it constantly available. The grave lords were responsible for the pit over which the bodies of dead kings were suspended for eighty days of dehydration, before transference to the royal mausoleum. The king's bodyguard was headed by a son or a grandson of a king as a security measure. The elimination of the head could not affect the succession; and he could be counted upon to report untoward circumstances. The Akan state was an orderly and settled state, riots were practically unknown as the political arrangements were ameliorative. Rebellions were naturally left to subject peoples, and much of the civic peace and contentment can be traced to the probably unique Akan divorce of rank and clan from power. Power was not oppressive of any class. The hierarchy of clan or rank could be different from that of power. Finally, the Akan society needs to be explained in terms of its spiritual egalitarianism.

Its Legal System

The Akans did not separate in different individuals or bodies the functions of the executive and the judiciary. These were cared for by the same bodies from the head of the family to the king in Council. The idea was that the body that promulgated law must know the intended import, and so was best placed to adjudicate between contending parties. This combination of functions was, of course, possible only when the functions of the judiciary were quite simple and not unduly complicated. In practice, the king's linguist acted as a sort of legal expert.

The distinction between civil and criminal offences was not very sharp. There was a simple method, that of swearing an oath against one's opponent, of converting a criminal offence into a civil one. The result of this was that punishments were often related not to the gravity of the explicit misdeed, but to the obstinacy with which the suit was pursued. There were no prisons, and the only forms of punishment inflicted were death or fines.

A court was summoned when a litigant compelled the defendant to appear by swearing an oath against him. Each oath carried a scale of penalties and forfeits appropriate to its gravity. An oath-swearing by the head of the king, or referring to a national catastrophe, could only be appeased by death. The fines imposed took cognisance both of the seriousness of the oath involved and the merits of the case being tried. The presiding judges had the option of deciding which party was to pay the oath fee. A temporarily worsted party could appeal by swearing the oath of a superior chief, right up to the king's oath. An oath could be sworn against even a chief, forcing him to answer a suit and be judged.

Deaths resulting from accidents had to be compensated for, and the heirs of the deceased had a right to name a sum. The sum agreed depended on the rank and position of the deceased.

A convicted murderer was sometimes allowed to execute himself either by explosion or by gunshot. Such a person was allowed a length of time of licence between his conviction and his execution.

Theft was punished by a fine, and, wherever possible, the restoration of the stolen goods. The physical punishment of the thief was administered by his own family. There was a wry capitalistic twist to the laws of theft. If a reasonable case could be made that a theft had deprived the aggrieved party of the chance of profit, compensation included both the capital value of the stolen goods and the profit which might have accrued. This law was usually applied to farm animals.

Marriage could be contracted by payment of a bride-price, sometimes as low as a pound, to the family of the prospective bride. The consent of the bride and the groom was not crucial, for, because the Akan family was extensive and integrated, the interest of more persons than the man and wife was concerned in marriage. And the advice offered by one's family was not arbitrary, but was based on considerations whose relevance one theoretically admitted oneself. One could not marry inside one's own clan; and one looked into the antecedents of the prospective companion, who must not be related to murderers or madmen. In so far as the family was a restriction on the individual's freedom to contract a marriage, the fairest way of putting the matter is to say that it precluded personal heroisms. It should however be admitted at the same time that when certain of the family restrictions were removed, the individual's range of the

81

possible increased, and this brought to him an enhanced sense of emancipation which is quite pertinent to the development of an industrialised society and the urban way of life.

The discovery that a bride had not entered married life as a virgin was a ground of divorce, and in such a case the husband could recover his bride-price on the score that the wife had contracted marriage under false pretences. If the accusation of premarital unchastity was false, the bride's father was able to summon the slanderous husband before a council, produce 'tokens of virginity', and demanded the payment of damages from him. The daughter could, if she wished, declare the marriage annulled.

Adultery was an offence committable only by a married woman. Her partner was fined. There was a cynical Akwamu chief who married all the women in villages he had conquered, went away for a year, and came back to collect the inevitable fines. An adulterous wife could be obtained as a wife by her partner if he paid adequate compensation to a consenting aggrieved husband, to cover the bride-price and expenses incurred to date. The woman was not allowed to consummate this new marriage immediately, and sometimes it was not consummated at all, the arrangement being a device to give her a status and diminish her disgrace. Adultery was naturally a ground of divorce.

The husband could only be in adulterous relation with another married woman. He could not be adulterous with a spinster, because marriage was polygamously defined.

Cruelty and neglect were grounds for separation. And desertion by the man for a period of three years conferred on the wife the right to remarriage.

Though marriage was polygamous in definition a man could not exercise this right without his wife's consent, which was signified customarily by the acceptance of a pacification fee. She had to accept this before the man could marry another woman. But he could install the other woman as a mistress without his wife's permission.

The principles of law were contained in the ideas of social organisation and the theory of man. Arbitrators often rested on the collective wisdom of the people, and in cases involving equity the apt invocation of a proverb or other accepted saying could quickly settle the matter unless countered with another apt saying. Otherwise, sayings and proverbs had the same effect as precedents.

The bearing of class on all this was quite incidental. One might recall the saying that nobility of birth could not be cooked and eaten; wealth was what mattered. As regards executions, a nobleman was encouraged to kill himself. As regards fines, he paid more heavily or was compensated more heavily. And as regards marriage, a man who married above his rank to the extent of the king's sisters was expected to take his life, and encouraged to do so, if he survived his wife.

Its Military Organisation

The military affairs of the Akans were under the overseership of a commander-in-chief who was always a war veteran. He was responsible for dividing levies among the chiefs of the provinces and the heads of the clans. He was responsible for maintaining the army at standard strength, for appointing officers and organising troops in battle-readiness. Next to the commander-in-chief was another veteran who was chief strategist, who planned campaigns and advised generals on the order of war. The grouping of troops in the field varied, but the victorious Ashantis arranged a battle formation looking roughly like an aeroplane. It was constructed in the following way. There was a central and prolonged column headed by the scouts, immediately followed by the advance guard. Behind these, the main body was massed. Then followed the commander-in-chief with his own warriors and aides-de-camp. Behind these came the carriers and accessories. Protecting these on the rear and facing the opposite direction was the rearguard. It was as though the central structure of the aeroplane should have two cockpits, both facing outwards, one in the front, the other at the back. The two wings were formed by ten columns, five on each side, departing from the main body and the commander-in-chief's men. These wing columns were made up of levies from principal towns. Next to the tip column in the left wing the king took his place when he went to war. The king was never in charge of the campaign even if he took part in it. Each body was responsible for its own supplies and combatant doctors.

A supply of runners were available for the purpose of communications, and the runners were in the commander-in-chief's entourage. Discipline was severe, and cowardice entailed death.

The Ashantis, who were incomparably the best Akan fighters, could field a hundred thousand men at a time. The army was a colourful sight even in the field. Each column had its own ensign, and when the chiefs accompanied the army, they were canopied under their huge umbrellas. These were ornate affairs of multi-coloured pieces of silk with frills of silver and gold, and embossed on top with a mass of gold. The chiefs were borne in their palanquins or sometimes phaeton-like chairs. These were of light wood or wicker-work studded with a large number of brass tacks and covered with tracery and carving.

The arms were long flintlock guns and blunderbusses, the cartridges for which were carried in girdles. These had attached to them leather or wooden cups into which powder was poured. The bullets were iron slugs. The soldiers slung over their shoulders a leathern pouch containing bark thread, bark crusts, iron pins, stones, and small snail-shells. The powder was loosely thrown into the barrel of the gun and was sometimes without wadding material. A handful of snail-shells or a piece of iron was dropped on the loose powder. This loose charge was then fired at close range.

Had the shooting technique of the Ashantis been better the Gold Coast would never have been a colony. As it was, the Ashantis defeated the British at least four times, and captured generals. H. M. Stanley, correspondent of the *New York Herald* in the 1870s, surmised that two thousand Ashanti warriors with one British officer could sweep the whole territory from Cape Coast to Timbuctoo at will, and, if they liked, also from Mandingo to Benin.

Once an army had taken to the field, it could not return to the capital without first seeking and obtaining permission to do so from the king in Council. The object of this was prudential. Large bodies of officered troops could not be allowed to enter at will a capital city with its civic authorities, without some caution. When a campaign had been successful the commander usually obtained permission to enter. If his mission had not been quite successful, permission was not always forthcoming immediately. Victories were celebrated publicly for two or three days, and another day was set aside for public mourning of casualties. Forty days after permission was granted, the army filed into the capital in review order. Each division, passing the king, fired a salute.

The public appearances of the king were occasions of pageantry. The appearance of the king was always preceded and announced by the talking drums. The talking drums are peculiar to Africa. They were not a means of signalling, but a method of actually talking. The drums tried to produce a voice. They were tympano-phonetic, not tympano-semantic. It is said that the news of the fall of Khartoum was known the same day to Africans in Sierra Leone. It was supposed to have been spoken by relays of talking drums.

Genealogies of kings, folklore as contained in proverbs, and praises were drummed out, as were messages to the materials from which the drums were made, the tree, the elephant's ear from which the membrane was obtained, the wood of the pegs, the creeper used to tie the skin. Apologies were made to these materials. Appeal was also made to the god of drumming. These were always the first messages on the drums. There also were prayers and references to *Onyankopon*. Alarms and insulting references about foes and foreigners were also drummed.

When the king of Ashanti received ambassadors, this was a state occasion. Thousands of persons, largely warriors, met the guests outside the capital, and completely engulfing them, led them in with intertwined music with skeins and threads from horn drums, rattles and *gong-gongs*. Musketry punctuated the pandemonious accompaniment regularly and massively. There were no end of leapfrog and other dancers. The whole ado was calculated to impress ambassadors with respect for Ashanti.

The war captains wore a cap displaying gilded ram's horns thrusting out in front. Plumes of eagle's feathers drooped down the sides, and the cap was fastened under the chin with bands of cowries. They wore vests of red cloth overlaid with charms in gold and silver, and loosely attached to the vests were colourfully embroidered cases. They carried whips made from the tails of animals, and knives. Farther down they wore baggy cotton trousers, and red boots which came high up and were secured at the top by strings or chains to a waistbelt. They had guns or bows and poisoned arrows. They also carried in their left hand small thrusting spears covered with red cloth and adorned with silk tassels. An Ashanti war captain was evidently a very expensive affair.

The ambassadors were gradually led through the capital. There was a high street with a number of minor streets leading off it. Along these streets, embanking them, were the Kumasi houses. The houses were squarish, and had large open porches in front like the stages in minor theatres. They were mainly one-storeyed. Designs were worked in clay and wood on the front façades and inside the courtyards. These patterns were mostly curvilinear. The rather simple ones were in the form of Greek r's. These were sometimes followed by one another at different levels and different inclinations across the breadth of the house where the floors met; very often their tails were collected together to form a swastika motif, the whole pattern being enclosed in a four-petal design. This ran along the base of the house to a height of some four feet. The doors were straight, and arches were usually reserved for the upper-storey windows.

The rooms were arranged round a courtyard which was also generally the parlour and kitchen, and also the playground of the little ones. This suggests the size of a traditional Akan house. They were typically mansions.

They were roofed with clay or tiles or turf, and the bathroom upstairs, equipped with a drainpipe. Some of these houses can still be seen today. They were built of adobe or bricks, burnt or unburnt. The beams were wooden, and the ceilings and walls were plastered over.

Cooking was done in earthen pots, over a stove consisting of three conical clay moulds set apart equiangularly. Fuel was dry sticks. A coal pot was also used. This consisted of an upper cylindrical portion filled with charcoal over a grate, and a lower portion with an air inlet. Spoons were of wood and food was eaten out of baked clay plates with the fingers. The plates were set on the floor or on a mat, and one sat on low stools.

Stools were the main kind of furniture. These were as artistic as they were functional. They consisted of an upper concave support for the seat, and an oblong base. The art was mainly shown in the intervening structure between the seat and the base. This structure was most attractively carved. Differences between kinds of stools were contained in their sizes and in the artistry of this intervening structure.

Internal decorations were mainly of brass objects and rich cloth. The Akans wore bark cloth, and the magnificent *kente* cloth worn exactly like a Greek robe. It was passed over the left shoulder, under the right armpit, and again over the left shoulder. An alternative way was to continue it round the back of the neck and over the right shoulder. Left-handed persons interchanged the shoulders. The bark cloth was dyed in vegetable dyes, and patterns were impressed upon them. The *kente* cloth was woven in long strips. It was either cotton, or a mixture of cotton and silk, or pure silk. The strips were beautified with the most gorgeous patterns and colours.

The houses were lit with oil lamps, and there was no system of public lighting.

The king and chiefs were the most resplendent personages. Their palanquins had curtains and pillows of rich crimson taffeta, and were surrounded by rich valance. Their umbrella canopies were topped by gold objects in the shape of animals, or a plain dome. Gold swords of state and maces were carried by officials. The king and chiefs wore fillets on their brows and temples, and these were bedecked with gold pads. Round their necks there hung obviously heavy sequences of gold necklaces of the most intricate artistry from which charms were suspended in small rectangular cases of gold and silver embroidery. Necklaces of Aggry beads running to their middles were also sometimes worn. Round the knees and ankles were bracelets of gold and beads. And they wore sandals of green, red and white leather with a V-shaped band reaching from the toe over the instep to the sides. On his breast the king wore a gold plate of leaf upon leaf. His fingers were clustered with heavy gold rings, and he wore a pair of gold castanets with which silence was signalled. He was flanked with musical instruments encased in gold of the thickness of cartridge paper. In short, gold simply ran riot.

The king was always a man of forceful personality, and always obviously proud but intensely refined. The speech of an elder was unfailingly a marvel of breeding and courtliness. When one was granted an audience, one could not ask permission to retire. One had to wait till the king signified the end of the audience.

Akan women originally wore little jewellery.

Its Literature

The question of a traditional Akan literature is a twofold one. First, there is the question, what is to be taken as constituting literature? This is a question being discussed today for the traditional African cultures. There is then the question, consequent on the first, of the possible literary content of the culture according to the decided acceptation.

It ought to be said at once perhaps that two types of definition or account are relevant here. A definition or an account may be said to be prescriptive, to set down antecedent conditions and limits to the nature of literature. Such an account in ideal uniquely settles the question, given any sequence of words, whether it constitutes literature or not. It is this kind of account that one encounters in dictionaries and the more enthusiastic sort of critical works. It usually stipulates individual authorship, a setting-down in writing, and esteem for beauty of form or emotional effect. Emotional effect is supposed to be achieved through the co-operation of matter and style. All these demands are indeed demands which directly affect the form and style of a literary piece of work. The last demand is, one supposes, responsible for the presumably apocalyptic sort of account given of literary criticism by personages like Belinsky, the nineteenth century Russian critic, according to whose perceptions criticism was aesthetics in motion. Literature has been produced for all sorts of reasons including the simple creative urge, and it has produced diverse effects founded in the emotions. The characters and situations and their treatment have been affected by a whole gamut of motives, some estimable, others not. The desire for vengeance (*Don Quixote*) has alternated with the desire to educate (*War and Peace*). It is quite unnecessary all the same that an author should have an axe to grind. Nevertheless the presence of a motive in the authorship of a literary piece controls the sort of emotional and aesthetic effect which it is calculated to produce, for it controls its style and images.

In terms of effects, literature may be put in two groups, practical and pure. Practical literature, including all didactic and protest literature, would be intended to influence human behaviour. Satiric poetry and conscience-stricken novels of the Dickens type, or even more recent novels about social climbers and their bestialities, would be examples of practical literature. Pure literature by contrast would not be intended to influence human behaviour. To achieve its purposes practical literature relies heavily on extra-semantic tools. It was probably exclusive familiarity with pure literature which led Newton to explain petulantly that poetry was 'ingenious nonsense'. It is obvious that his enjoyment of literature would have been incomplete even if he had taken pleasure in nonsense.

The insistence on individual authorship is perhaps most suitable, of all *genres* of literature, to the novel. Co-operative effort, if simultaneous, is possible here, as in the link-up between Dickens and Wilkie Collins. But the intricacy of the development of plot in an integrated novel, even including a slice-of-life novel, calls for individual execution. A stream-of-consciousness novel could be built up or even modified by a team, but, in general, even this is—for better or for worse—best written through individual authorship. It is evident that with certain sub-classes of poems, including the ballad, it is possible for successive generations to change incidents and refrains in order to preserve the spirit of the work and the topicality of its incidents. Some literary types lend themselves more easily to unsettled and composite authorship than others do.

For this reason, a definition of literature which lays indiscriminate emphasis on individual authorship could be unduly narrow and restrictive. Even without relating it to literature transmitted through oral traditions, one could argue that such a prescriptive definition, clamping down literature, as it does, in its strait-jacket, would be entirely insensitive to the startling reproductive aspect of literature which is almost like scenery after rain, and to the achievement of analysis in a synthetic picture, its provision of both a focus and a perspective for problems and questions; and it would also be completely flustered by new departures in technique and form, or even subject, in literature. It would be quite unequipped for coping with the idiosyncrasies of literary movements, and so be impervious to much that marks genius.

To understand the accrescent contribution of successive individuals to the same piece of literature in the Akan oral tradition one must bear in mind the functions of oral traditions in that society. In passing, one may cite the process of emendation in written literature, which inevitably results in a form of a work that owes elements of merit or demerit to scholars. The principle of *lectio difficilior* inevitably leads to incorrect editions.

The oral tradition among the Akans covered a number of subjects. These had to do mainly with wars and migrations, genealogies and royal successions as well as clan-successions. The uses to which this kind of material might be put are sacred, national, or legalistic. When they are put to sacred uses, they deal with the origin of the ethnic group, with notable and specially revered ancestors. They are here used to renew the solidarity and unity of the group. The style of the presentation of the material is naturally here highly evocative, and resort is made to high-sounding praise-names. When they are put to national uses, the names of ancestors revered specially for their virtues, in which those of the community are seen, are mentioned, their virtues put before the people for the guidance of their conduct and their appraisal of situations. Indeed, the names of the great ones were commonly given to children apart from the formal method of naming, in the hope that the illustrious virtues would be repeated in them, apart from the influences which their weekday of birth, uniquely signified in the children's weekday names, were thought to have. When oral traditions were used in a legalistic way, they were in the nature of historical material for settling questions about rights and justified interests. Heads of families were expected to be well-versed in the history of their families.

So far nothing that is clearly literature has been treated of, though the presentation of the type of material mentioned above admits of literary devices. Raconteurs were able to improvise on any of the above themes, on both military and civic exploits, and in order that effect should not be lost, profuse use was made of the literary qualities of the language including exaggeration, association and suggestion, and new and stylised images. Dupuis mentions that the Ashantis had composed a song in 1807 revealing as only one of their glories how a river of blood had been forced to flow from Miassa, lamented capital of Assin, to the Prah. This kind of detail was usually surrounded by a large number of heroic images and turns of phrase. It was open to a raconteur to change the images handed down to him in a composition, and even surround salient details in his account with more local and topical allusions. A raconteur revealed his verbal virtuosity in the way in which he adorned the bare substance of his recitative. The account as presented and publicly received was therefore already affected by purely literary creativity, even if it was not entirely an individual creation. During a public presentation, the thought and emotion of audiences were kindled, and emotional participation was secured. This was often made easier to secure by musical accompaniment. The need to adapt musical aids to the proceedings without submerging the verbal account forced the raconteur to seek musical qualities in his words. Thus there was a public exploitation of sound and semantic value for aesthetic effect. When this was successful, the sound of the word and its association, and so its evocative power, were deeply enriched by the musical accompaniment. The whole procedure gave the traditional literature its semblance of communal drama. This was, however, a superficial aspect. The important thing was not the refrain or foreknowledge of the public of what was coming but the individual raconteur's own virtuosity. Though the subjects treated—the state of the society, the position of the chief in it, the relationship of man to society, and the family to society, the relationship of the world of man to the world of spirit, the communal emotion and attitudes to virtues, origins, military and civic triumphs—could occur in various disciplines from theology to sociology, the manner of their treatment by trained artists turned some of the results among the Akans into literature.

One has to admit that when literature is orally transmitted, its shape is greatly affected, for detailed and sustained characterisation becomes impossible, and realism tends to crumble into legend. Plot becomes rather emasculated, and its intricacies are concentrated into the clever moves found in trickster stories. These were collected around particular animals though human and semi-divine tricksters too had these picaresque anecdotes clustered round them. There was the Hare in East Africa and Nigeria, the Tortoise in Nigeria—also transported to Cuba—Anansi the spider in Ghana, Liberia, Sierra Leone, also transported to Jamaica and Dutch Guiana. It is no doubt the same as the 'Aunt Nancy' of South Carolina. Of human and semi-divine tricksters, the Zulus had Hankanyana, the Dahomeans Yo, the Yorubas Eshu and Orunmila, the Akans Amamfi. Even if plot suffers, however, dialogue need not be affected, and here was where the literary tradition of the trickster stories could suffer most change. Ungifted storytellers did their best to remember dialogue, gifted ones remembered themes, and like the spider spun their dialogue out of their own internal fertility. The picturation of situation is another aspect of oral literature which obviously suffered fluctuations, and the length of stories would tend to vary with the ability of their tellers.

The fact that oral literature was thus continually renewed and changed, normally for the better, tended to develop the Akan languages as literary languages. To this day they are markedly literary. There is perhaps no one reason for this. Mankind has been moving from a metaphysical apprehension of the world to a naturalistic one. That this is the historical movement and not the reverse, as Tylor seems to have thought in his ideas about the origin of the notion of spirit and the supernatural, is supportable by considerable evidence. Indeed, it could be said of Thales that his revolution consisted in his insistence to the pre-Socratic Greeks that to explain nature it was sufficient to cite nature, and unnecessary to have recourse to the supernatural.

The literary qualities of a language indicate the extent of the freedom of the creators of literature, for the need to conform is greater in neutral and naturalistic languages. The manner of presenting scientific data is a sombre example. Literature is a function of the richness and imaginative litheness of a language. The converse too is true, at least to the extent that literature purges language. The Akan storyteller was not in any way shackled by his family connections. His family certainly did not make any attempts to do his composition for him, nor were even his titles recommended to him. The tradition of the Mastersingers is of all European developments probably the one that comes nearest to the Akan situation.

The Akan literary output can be arranged in four groups, suggested by J. R. Nketia. First, there is the purely oral literature which was recited and not sung. This was spoken in connection with chiefship at state functions, and was replete with allusions to martial glories and renowned victories of particular chiefs. References were also made to their civic ingenuity and prowess. It centred on persons rather than ideas, coming near the latter only in the treatment of inter-personal relationships. There was, secondly, the recitative which was half-spoken and half-sung. This comprised dirges and hunters' songs of celebration. The references and allusions made could be grouped around a few themes, usually comprising ancestors, particular individuals, and the fortunes of the family. Third, there was lyric poetry, in which song was used as a vehicle for poetry. A great deal of Akan poetry is sung. Included in this were worshipful statements, ceremonial statements, and the individual deliverances of poets. It was, apart from the proverb, saw, or apophthegm, the other means used for stylised exhortation, and other didactic purposes. Fourthly and lastly, there were the messages of horns and drums which by their pitch, turn of phrase, and economy of expression, were literary.

Very few of the pieces falling into the four groups justified the preoccupation of the old anthropologists with proverbs as exclusive specimens of African literature. The proverbs were in fact aphoristic sayings enjoying a traditionally handed-down currency, but were at the same time rigid in their form. They were usually intended statements of fact with the possibility of moral application. The enjoyment of them usually arose from their brevity and their protean powers of interpretation. Their rigidity completely contrasted with the freedom of invention of the raconteur. The Akans did not count proverbs among their literary pieces. Nor did they include the proverbial sayings which were not completely rigid and could quite permissibly be misquoted, and varied with tense and person. Wellerisms too existed in abundance; they were in the form of couplets in which a speaker is ostensibly mentioned and quoted (like the one about what the spider said to the fly. The goat, too, says that if success with females qualified one for the throne, he would be a king in a palanquin.) There were also aetiological tales explaining, for example, how the elephant got its tail. These too were not counted. There was an ambiguous attitude however, to fables conveying moral lessons, which were pedagogic devices rather than literary pieces. Cantefables, mixtures of verse and narrative, were however accepted.

The proverbial sayings were not necessarily short and terse, indeed they were on occasion quite expansive, sounding more like stories than like those self-subsistent concentrates which genuine proverbs are. These proverbial sayings are widespread in Africa and even their themes bear strong similarity to one another from place to place. While the Yorubas say the world has come to a pretty pass when an egg drops into an earthen pot and it is the pot that breaks, the Akans have similar feelings about the lizard which dropped from the top of the coconut tree, and, nodding its head up and down, asked the earth if the earth felt dizzy. One supposes that the English similarly say 'the dog it was that died'. Here in this domain, too, the pragmatic spirit finds scope and the insulation of social arrangements from private emotion is stressed. Thus, the Yorubas have noticed that one does not become so mad at one's head that one wears one's hat on one's buttocks. The whimsical absurdity of such sayings is doubtless a source of pleasure and titillation to the imagination.

The trickster stories were recreational and educative. A catalogue of likely tricks were set out in story form and successful counter-moves to them were described. They were sometimes used to insist on justice and resist arbitrariness while maintaining courtesy. An alternative way of doing the same thing was to place impossible conditions on impossible demands. Among the Ganda, a person ordered by the ruler to make a human being asked as raw materials for a thousand loads of charcoal made of human hair and a hundred pots of tears. And when the Tortoise was asked in the Cameroons to fetch water in a basket, he politely but firmly asked for a carrying strap of smoke. Respect for authority was in this way easily combined with the integrity of justice. The merit of this device lay in its avoidance of openly personalised conflict with constituted authority. Instead of a blunt refusal and disobedience, authority was presented with seeming cooperation which was in fact destructive of the idea of the given task. Among the Akans, Anansi the spider had a similar method for dealing with impertinence and humbug. There was a tyrant who could not bear to be contradicted. He put to death all those whom, by his tall stories and idiotic requests, he had provoked into gasps of unbelief. One day, Anansi visited him and withstood all the provocations. Anansi invited him back and hid himself, having told his children how to handle him. The tyrant did well at first but soon broke down, contradicted, and was set upon. Some of the things said were: once when he asked for water to drink from the cooler pot, he was told that the top layer belonged to Anansi who was away, the middle part to an aunt who would be furious, and only the bottom portion to the children who could not reach it without disturbing the other portions. Trying to find out where Anansi was, he was told that in trying to pluck a fruit from a tree with his penis, he had broken it in several places, witness the seven red marks on the floor, and he had gone to fetch medicines.

Some of these stories were designed to emphasise the superiority of brilliance over steadiness. For example, the

African Tortoise won his race against the Hare not by toiling upward in the night while his companion slept, but by planting in the shrubs along the route several tortoises like him, the last of whom stirred himself to the tape at a suitable time. The unity of the clan and the value of co-operative effort are also involved in this story.

That the Akans developed a tradition of literary criticism is evident from their instigation of raconteurs to greater and greater perfection in arrangement, image, and delivery. Following the principle *de gustibus non est disputandum* with any zeal soon exposes one to charges of vulgarity. It is by no means always an accomplishment to differ from tastes communally accepted as refined. One supposes that pleading the quotation in excuse does not diminish Tolstoy's oddity in rating Shakespeare on a par with Walter Scott. The vagaries of literary taste do not altogether escape discipline, and it is perhaps the order and fastidiousness which the body of critical opinion introduces into literature which has led some to call criticism a nagging, fault-finding activity.

It is possible to a very limited extent to gather from the languages themselves something of the literary canon, for every language itself entails certain criteria of excellence and picturesqueness. For example, the same ideas which when expressed in a certain way in a particular language will be humorous, could at best only be grotesque in another language. Likening a colleague's face to the inside of a Hades bricklayer's pocket, or to a faded Hades 'Rule Britannia' penny, is an unfailing way of blowing laughter on the lips of youths. In English, its speaker might be complimented on his imagination, but hardly on his gifts for humorous expression.

Naturally, it cannot be the whole canon of literary appreciation which the language itself suggests, for much is also conceptual, and includes ideas about the relation of one individual to another, the relationship of an individual to society and the spiritual. One finds that characterisation, the limning of the individual in the round, was notably absent in the traditional Akan literature. This has an explanation in the very conception of society and of the individual. Since society was thought of as comprising individuals with antecedent duties and responsibilities, the three-dimensional individual, completely subsistent, and a distinct atom, was non-existent. Literature did not therefore portray him. The social contract was not merely false of Akan society; with reference to it, it was nonsensical, for, even before a man was born, his spiritual factors belonged to specific ethnic groups. Character types were therefore more interesting to Akan literature than characters in the round. It is probably this different tradition of type-characterisation, typical of African literature, which has made three-dimensional characterisation by African novelists in English and French so far a failure. Their characters have tended to be flat and canvassy. Involved in this is naturally the whole question, for them, of approach.

In a communalistic society, not everything was communally done, though many things were done with intention for the communal good. Akan literary criticism was not seriously engaged in by the public except the older heads; criticism was largely contentedly left to the producers of literature themselves. It took the form of establishing literary conceptions, explaining them to apprentices, and thereby trying to make them prevail. Their central concern was with particular, stylised expressions, whose repeated occurrence never failed to be applauded, and methods and techniques of construction and output. Gifted producers of literature brought their talents to bear on these elements, and their talents were first released and exercised in criticism, in an ordered sum of their constantly-aware response to established pieces maturely run through, of evaluations and comparisons, and therefore also of shifting standards—for comparison in literature has the effect of shifting standards. In this way, in Akan literature, classicism came to be combined with romanticism; the makers of literature, brought up on the basis of the existing masterpieces, set up a code of standard and level of style for their own works, but in their works became also, each of them, a law-giver and a phoenix.

But if our raking up and study of the oral literature can provide a foundation for the education of the traditional criticism, it must at the same time be realised that in its presentation we cannot ignore the results of our contact with European literature and the attitudes of critical evaluation germane to it. If even in the presentation of this we must take note of our contact with Europe, then it becomes almost self-evident that when we write some of our modern literature in English or French, to some extent we thereby also write for European audiences. The problem of approach here becomes a little involved. The African novelists writing in English and French themselves declare it to be their purpose to write for their cosmopolitan African public. Unless there is something African, which the normal run of English and French literature does not provide, and which the African public, even when cosmopolitan, needs, one cannot understand why the African novelists should feel it their proper mission to address themselves to the African public. Achebe has a sense of this mission. With, also, the possible exception of Camara Laye, the African novelists have not tried hard to satisfy it. Instead, including Amos Tutuola with his often incomprehensible idiosyncratic dialect, they have eagerly accepted the moulds offered to them externally by European critics, and have crammed themselves into these moulds, driven neither by inspiration nor even by conviction. The result is that the Tutuola enchantment is already palling, and Cyprian Ekwensi is doing well with the Nigerian Broadcasting Corporation. The torch has passed into the hands of late starters like Achebe, who continues to be more and more promising.

There are, broadly, two ways in which the African novelists can cater for their specified African public. They can bring into their language their own vernaculars. By this, one has in mind turns of phrase and suggestive local idioms characteristic of one's vernacular. A practical way in which this question turns up is in the treatment of an African rustic in literature written in the first instance in English or French. There is a glib saying that the common people are everywhere the same. Though true within very narrow limits, this is a statement which might well obscure what a little reflection is in fact adequate to show. African rustics are different in many important respects from their English and French counterparts. In Europe, it is the Irish and the pre-revolutionary Slav peasants who are most similar to them. To say that social conditions and geography can account for much of a people's character is only to repeat a commonplace of sociology. The proverbial dourness of the Scot is traditionally imputed partly to 'Caledonia, stern and wild', partly to the rigours of Presbyterian discipline. Hereditary indigestion may of course always have something to do with it. Hence even on grounds of social conditions and sociology alone, not to mention those of metaphysical upbringing, a difference in genius is to be expected between African rustics and English and French ones. The English language is part of the expression of the genius of the English people, and its abhorrence of generalised rules admirably reflects the empiricism of the English spirit. In any case one can hardly think of rustic dialect in English without thinking of the dialect of English rustics. In the African novel in English, the local rustic might easily be made to speak like English rustics. The idioms, the humour, the ethic, will then be those of the English rustic. And what goes for English goes for French. But, obviously, it is perfectly possible to describe an Eskimo in Chinese without violence to realism. Descriptive realism is not, by the way, the same as reproductive verisimilitude. Whereas the former is appropriate to the essayist, it is the latter at which the novelist aims.

Admittedly, it is proper for our new African novelists to do for Africa what Hardy and Lawrence did for Britain. They can do this by putting their vernacular behind their English and their French, by writing of the mass of traditional Africa as though they were translating into English or French. The freshness of their work in European languages will rest squarely on those modes of the hypothetical original which can survive in the hypothetical translation. Their vernacular will reflect moral attitudes, idiom, stylistic mannerisms, personalities and situations. What a situation is for a novelist should be how a situation is grasped, and when two languages differ in their ability to state things with generality, to take an example from the differences between African languages and certain European languages, it is evident that a novel about traditional Africans has to show finesse in the construction and building up of situation. It is features like this which will make modern African literature in European languages African, and not the simple fact that the literature has been written by Africans.

The type of humour which can be ascribed to the traditional African is another element which is firmly rooted in the vernacular, and is nourished by the bizarre and the fantastic.

The second way in which the African novelists can cater for their African public is by exploiting the condition of their societies, the compresence of the traditional and the various eclectic elements from the West and the Middle East, the fluidity of our present, the confrontation of cultures, the break-up of old institutions, apart from picturing the mentalities, the beliefs, the customs, the wit, solidity, traditional puritanism, aristocratic courtesies, and generous hospitality. These could sustain any number of novels and plays. If the African novelists and playwrights showed enough sensitivity to the vast field that lay before them, the 'man of two worlds', boring as he tends to be, would be cut down to size, and would not haunt them so persistently. The man of two worlds, the man who has been exposed in no consistent or radical fashion to a *milieu* which is different from that to which he belongs, though the latter continues to surround him, is a truly displaced man. His mastery of the new culture is not comprehensive enough, it is selfconscious, and, such as it is, it is generally in conflict with *mores* into which he was born, and which he has never truly uprooted from his system. His is cultural ambiguity, not cultural ambivalence, for it is characteristically accompanied by mis-givings. These misgivings, this tension, this near-neurosis, can be most tragic. The man of two worlds, uncomfortably striding both, is the real displaced man.

As to Akan literature itself, it continues to prosper and derive advantage from modern literacy. The ability to write exercises a profound influence on the modern literature in Akan. For one thing, it makes expansiveness in literature possible. This is in direct contradistinction to the terse piquancy of the traditional literature. Expansiveness has made possible the detailed prose-cution which makes three-dimensional characterisation easier. It has also bestowed visual as distinct from sonal qualities on the poetry through its setting-out in print. It can now be read in silence with enjoyment. Literacy has also made forthcoming more personal statements in poetry, for its audience is now atomised. Where the old poets gave their personal expression to truths educed from the communal world-view, and also to the communal emotion and ethic, the Akan poet today gives more and more his own statement of his private apprehension of the world, and of his private emotions and ethic. Even so, there are some modern poets like J. H. Nketia who express communal feelings in their poetry, which is inspired by the living Akan traditions. In illustration, I cite a rather free translation of two excerpts from Nketia's Akan poetry. The first is from a piece called *First Steps*.

> And I saw a bird-child searing through the air
> His mouth sealed by the twigs that it carried
> Yonderward over the sea, to give to Yaa Manu
> For the washing of her soul.
>
> And did the bird-child arrive and was not seen of Noah?
> Did I not see the wind to poise a rock-piece
> To threaten the bird-child that rubber-balled
> Along the water-way, fretting the wild-boar
> Whom it nagged?
>
> And did the rock home on the bird, and the bird-child
>   not die? . . .
> The house that I build is ravished by the slime-fungus.
> The basket that I weave is o'vercome by the mud-slush,
> Farm of Fosu, the Father, falls into a bush of thorns . . .

The second is from a piece called *The Moon*.

> Was it not recently that, squatting on a hill,
> I saw the Moon set out from the village,
> Roll to the market place, fanfare herself?
> Traveller, who has conspired with night,
> Butterflies pin-point her way and fan her;
> Some all-hail her, while others sweep her route,
> A few put torches just before her step,
> Many lie ahead, behind, to left and right.
> All tongues trill.

Children of Mother Earth, woman of Thursday,
Prank about in the open light.
Elders talk and children prick their ears.
But traveller, bird of passage, thou Moon,
Squatting on the hill I can see you no more.

Who snatched the white light from my hands,
Who will show me where the Moon has gone?
Where shall I place my foot that blessing may not pass me by?
Where shall I plant my seat that I may not see change?
In tribulation, are there cyclic changes?
One day, one night?

Hold! Go back. Tell all the tribes.
The Moon is not dead; she went, but has now come back.
Let the old make talk, and let the children play.
Sit and squat the soothsayer upon the hill,
And gaze into spaces. The princess steps
Again into her footprints. She has set out from the village,
And night feels sullen.

The love with which you love me alone o'ercomes me.
That is what I prize. When I squat upon the hill
And cannot see your face, I shall know that by my side,
Your love squats upon the hill. When I
Squat upon the hill and cannot see your face
I shall know that I am not forgot.

In these two pieces, the tragic temperament of the Akan is well mirrored. The fact that laughter is often on the lips of an Akan is itself evidence of his melancholy. Laughter is melancholy as comedy is tragic. The source of the Akan's laughter is very often in his apprehension of the bizarre. The merely incongruous is a little too weak to provoke mirth, and too often succeeds in inciting impatience and shortening temper. The tragic temperament of the Akan reveals itself in occasional attitudes of the face which evince an atavistic kind of suffering and grief. At least, it is nourished by the whole of the Akan metaphysic and the principles underlying their social organisation. The belief that we belong to a society to which also belong in a non-visible habit the spirits of our ancestors, who are constantly milling around us, and the belief that we are all here to fulfil a destiny, are not calculated to induce levity of mind. Preoccupation with the spirituality of man seems everywhere to have bred a tragic type of mind. Spirituality-theories can, of course, take different forms, and even humanism, one supposes, by discovering in the human condition a certain intrinsic moral value, becomes a spirituality-theory of man. Not surprisingly therefore the unhumorous earnestness of many protagonists of humanism has around it an unmistakable tragic flavour.

The melancholy of the Akans was probably summed up in their ideals of a largely reverent attitude towards spiritual matters and a profound seriousness about the conduct of earthly life.

If one does not give a prescriptive account of literature, one might give a descriptive one. Here, one assumes an undisputed body of literature and studies it. One advantage of this procedure is that it is always open, and so quite prepared for the new possibilities of art which a major maker of literature might introduce. However strong tradition might be, it must leave room for the individual talent. Minimally literature may be said to be a body of experience of sensitive men and women, given flesh through the imaginative use of language, and able to kindle an appraising response of thought and emotion in its public. By this token literature becomes an art.

Its Ethics and Metaphysics

Most philosophical theories can usually be stated in a few sentences. A great deal of philosophical writing consists, according to a colleague, J. E. Wiredu, of an anticipation of the objections of half-wits and replies thereto. Much also comprises explanations of the statement of the theories themselves, and of course arguments for them. The absence of a body of writing among the Akans does not in itself, therefore, mean the absence of philosophical ideas. Griaule and Balandier have put questions to sage Africans and elicited from them statements and views which are without doubt philosophical. The Abbé Alexis Kagame wrote a doctoral thesis on the concept of being among the Ruanda-Urundis. Father Placide Tempels sketched the world view and the ethics consequent on this among the Balubas of the Congo. Dr Danquah in Ghana has done extensive work on the concept of God among the Akans. Intense as some of these works have been, they have been quite sporadic in incidence, and have not been quite clearly seen as forming efforts in a recognisable field of African philosophical speculation.

There are, of course, two main aspects of such a field, the public aspect and the private. Workers in the field can find all over Africa specimens of what might be called a public philosophy, usually tracing out the theoretical foundations of the traditional society. There is also the private philosophy, however, which is more the thinking of an individual than a laying-bare of the communal mind. Without any doubt, much of Kagame's work and also Griaule's is of this latter kind. Griaule, it might be said, found in his blind hunter an individual African philosopher rather than a repository of the public philosophy.

At the same time, the question whether there is an African philosophy must be distinguished from the question whether there are African philosophers. Though a negative answer to the latter implies a negative answer to the former, a positive answer to it leaves the former question still open. The question of the existence of an African philosophy is not a 'uniqueness' question. There is no reason why, in order that there should be an African philosophy, it has to be different from every other philosophy. It is sufficient that philosophy should occur in Africa such that it is not derived from outside Africa.

Some of the problems raised in philosophy elsewhere have answers in African thought. One might take theory of knowledge as an example. Theory of knowledge, speaking roughly, concerns the conditions of knowledge in general, an attempt to fix the limits of the human understanding and its avenues to knowledge of different types, a type of knowledge being in fact constituted a type in virtue of the avenue which the understanding has to it. But theory of knowledge also concerns itself with particular items of knowledge, especially those the application of whose concept-term is also an appraisal situation. Professor Ryle's success-verbs come under this heading. But so do many terms which feature in ethics, like voluntary, excuse, deliberate, willed, intention, *et cetera*. The concept of motive alone, for example, involves the concept of a reasonable man. Whether a man is said to have a motive or not does not depend crucially on his own admissions or the fruit of his introspection. He is not thought to be a privileged observer of his own motives. What motives he is credited with or accused of depend on the general features of his behaviour and the public idea of the reasonable man in his situation. But the public image of the reasonable man is itself heavily infected by the organisation of society and its theoretical foundations. This is why the reasonable man so nearly corresponds everywhere to the ethical man. But if the image and deportment of the reasonable man in being reasonable, depend on the kind of society in which he is located, it is clear that resolutions of ethical problems which are in fact only quasi-theoretical are going to reflect differences in types of societies. To conclude the example, even if catalogues of motives are the same, the ascription of motives will be affected by the theory of society current. Philosophical positions concerning them will show parallel differences. The resort of linguistic philosophers to what we say or do is not, therefore, shortsighted. This is where relativism might affect philosophy.

The limits of the human understanding and of knowledge have been differently drawn by different peoples, and the cleavage between rationalism and empiricism reflect such a difference. This kind of difference does not often reveal itself in the vocabulary, but more often in redefinitions and explications. In the rationalist traditions, for example, in order to explain one thing in terms of another, one must be able to establish an inference from the one to the other. Mere invariant succession is inadequate, and so far from providing an explanation, it itself calls for one. Hence some accounts which in an empiricist tradition would be of the nature of an explanation would in a rationalist tradition be neither correct nor incorrect, but the wrong kind of thing to call an explanation at all. This kind of difference over the notion of explanation already indicates an acceptance of some general concepts and classification of experience. And this introduces metaphysics. The fundamental classification of experience *prima facie* offers various possibilities. The study of philosophical models is itself parasitic on this *prima facie* possibility, for what a philosophical model presents is an epistemological ontology, the general categories of being and their constitution, which form a conceptual framework for apperception of the world. In the West, the bifurcation into matter and spirit is no longer a burning question, the possibility that quality might be founded on quantity causes few nightmares, the explication of spirit into dispositions, and minds into abilities, the founding of individual identity on characteristics of body and relations of bodies, these are philosophical delicacies which strike sourly on the Akan philosophical palate. The questions are philosophical, and so equally are the verbal reactions to them.

Concerning spirit and matter, we have said that the Akans drew a distinction, but did not regard the two categories as being co-ordinate; that the Akans distinguished a number of spiritual factors in a man, that though a body could be identified through physical characteristics, an individual did not so hold his personal identity. Personal identity was traced to the identity of the *Okra*. Clan identity was traced to the *mongya*. The *sunsum* was held to be responsible for character, and the identity of character depended on the exclusion of possession by an alien *sunsum*. Thus, a non-dispositional view of character was held in Akan thinking. Moral defects were spiritual flaws, and almost sinful. They were thought to be removable by, so so to say, spiritual surgery.

Because morality was so based on metaphysical beliefs, the ethics of the Akans was rationalistic. Since the moral sanctions were spirit-regarding, with a little casuistry they came to accommodate much that was barbarous and cruel. They are the same metaphysical colour notwithstanding, which explains the sense of outrage that the Akans had about moral aberrations. Traditionally, it was not merely a disgrace to be immoral, it was almost sinful, for immorality was held to jeopardise spiritual welfare. The rationalistic, and so absolutist nature of the ethics, also explains the reluctance to admit degrees of gravity of the same misdeed. The classification of the misdeed was held to be formal and defining, and so to admit of no degrees. Punishment did not often in consequence reflect any differences in degree of seriousness of the offence in its severity. An empiricist attitude towards crime and punishment works for humaneness in the latter.

The distinction between spirit and matter, the most fundamental in Akan metaphysics, is reinforced by their distinction between quality and property. Whereas property might come to be founded on the quantitative, in Akan thinking no room was left for quality also being resolvable.

Still philosophy was never scholastic among the Akans, and might Spinozistically be said to be the idea of that of which society was the body. Just as the traditional society has receded into the Akan village, so has the traditional public philosophy. This philosophy fixed the Akan religion and the Akan morality, and indeed often inspired Akan law. The souls of men were members of a spiritual republic, sojourning for a while in flesh, and the rites that an individual had to perform, like those of the washing of the soul, were intended to be phenomenal marks of spiritual states, in order that the society at large might thereby be afforded an insight into its condition as a spiritual entity.

Akan law could be conceived as a sort of supplement to ethics. The retribution that followed moral evil was often slow to come, and when it did come, it was held to express either the displeasure of Nyame, who was said to abhor evil, or the atonement which a troubled spirit wreaked on itself. This sort of retribution, because it could be slow in coming, was not always clearly enough seen to be connected with evil-doing. Wicked men might therefore be tempted to great activity. To limit this, systems of man-made law were created which prescribed visible punishment, lest the wicked should seek to profit from the slowness and long-suffering of Nyame or the indulgence of one's own soul. Naturally, law had also a purely temporal inspiration.

Social rules were more or less informal and further regulated the association between people. Without being completely rigid, they tended to confirm status.

It is with the culture that I have barely described that the Western culture has unilaterally interacted. Very few elements of Akan culture have been transmitted to the West. On the other hand, Western cultural influence has been channelled along imperialist, commercialist and missionary lines. As long as the imperialistic design might be thwarted by the unifying and binding power of culture, it became of interest to imperialism to weaken this culture. The initial outrages towards the Golden Stool of Ashanti could only be explained in this way. As long as the Golden Stool existed and was in their keeping, the Ashantis, it was thought, were bound to defend their nation against all aggression. With the entry of Rattray into the field, he quickly persuaded the Colonial Office that any direct move against the Golden Stool was bound to be lustily resisted. When Ashanti was settled, the women made a silver stool, not out of a feeling of subjection, but out of friendship, and presented it to Princess Mary. A passage of the speech delivered to Governor Guggisberg by the Queen Mother of Ashanti went like this.

'We pray the great God Nyankopon, on whom men lean and do not fall, whose day of worship is a Saturday, and whom the Ashantis serve just as she [Princess Mary] serves Him, that He may give the King's child and her husband long life and happiness, and finally, when she sits upon this silver stool, which the women of Ashanti have made for their white Queen Mother, may she call us to mind.'

The missionaries too were guilty of their own acts of vandalism. Thinking that the Akans and other Africans worshipped their objects of art, they collected a great many such objects with great assiduity and consigned them to the flames. It is a miracle that some specimens have survived.

A major vehicle of westernisation was, of course, the formal school. It was ridiculously easy for it to take place for the reason that the formal school was largely unknown to Africa. Though it therefore totally lacked conditions from which to grow naturally, there was, at the same time, little in the *status quo* with which the formal school could be incompatible. The prestigious benefits attending a Western education in an African setting decidedly seduced quite a few persons, some of whom marvellously had their nationalism thereby only made doubly articulate. The representatives of the metropolitan countries carried their culture into the colonies, and those of their subjects who were absorbed into the new administrative and new cultural whirl sought a place in the new glowing cultural sun. The reorientation started in the schools where even the folktales children were told were other folks' tales, not theirs. The standards of passable behaviour and possible ideals embedded in these tales could not always be assumed to be local, and in this way, from the beginning, children were encouraged to live, in addition to an outward life, an inner life that was apart from that of their relations and people; to lose their feeling for that complex from which they had sprung. They were instead encouraged to exploit the startling abilities of the European, his technology, his resourcefulness, his cheeky but rewarding curiosity about nature, and the impression this had made on Africans, in a bid to divert to themselves in a vicarious way something of the reputation of the white man. This was so much accepted in the north of Nigeria, for example, that Africans who today do the jobs Europeans did yesterday are there called white men.

Through the orientation of the formal school, a great opportunity for enriching African cultures was thrown away, for there was no organised and purposeful drive to borrow and adapt, urged by a sense of needs and capacities, a process which would have meant an interweaving of elements of Western cultures with African cultures in an understandable and digestible form.

By means of commercial activity, new tastes and new processes of economic activity were introduced; with these came Western systems of law and mechanisms of government. These did not however seek thoroughly to transform the whole scene; the latter were kept at a minimum, while the former thrived in a riotous way.

Though the vandalism of missionaries has been referred to, artistic expression is perhaps the side of the traditional life which was least shaken. Dance music and literature have continued in strength; and even though the vulgar tourist art has been taking the place of traditional sculpture, the talent for the latter continues to be in evidence.

The patronage which the traditional plastic artists enjoyed was given by chiefs and heads of families, and also by the priesthood. Religious and secular art could be distinguished not so much according to their content as according to their use. Religious art may be said to have included figures and figurines of gods and ancestors. The masks which were put to a magical use would have occupied a role half-way between the religious and the secular. Secular art itself was mainly decorative and informative. It was used to adorn a person or the home, and sometimes to signify rank or a clan.

Mention has been made of the decoration in architecture and on furniture. Mention has also been made of the artistry involved in gold and silver ornaments, the outfits of chiefs offering a startling example of it. The ancestral figures were decorative most of the time, and were put to a magical use only on those anniversaries when the ancestors were invoked. The ancestor figures were not meant to trap the spirits of ancestors in order to harness them. In any case, they did not look like the ancestors. They were only a focus for their presence when they were invoked.

The themes of the art with which we are concerned tended to be connected with origins and life, and included the gods, reproductive forces, usually mother and child, ancestors and forebears. There were masks for fertility rites, and symbolic designations of clans in the shape of plants and animals.

The problems which led to the selection of themes were theoretical ones, for the conservation of institutions had mapped out almost automatic remedies for practical ills. Since the society, from its spiritual orientation, could be loosely said to be sacred, the theoretical problems tended to bear on the nature of gods and other spirits, man's relationship to them, the symbolic designation of the spiritually interwoven clan, the provision of a *locus* for departed ancestral spirits, the provision of nature for man in agriculture and birth, and the exploration of disease.

As the Akans could not write, they expressed their philosophico-religious ideas through art, through the timeless, immemorial, silent, and elemental power so characteristic of African traditional art. Indeed this is the main reason why it was not life-like in a representational sense. Forms had to be distorted. In art, there was a moral-philosophical preoccupation which led it to portray forces of the world, and to portray a force it was essential that it should not be treated like something assimilated, and consequently like something overcome, as the rendering of it in life-like figures would have been. When the purpose of a work of art required it to be life-like, it was life-like enough. The Ashanti wooden *maidens*, which epitomise the Ashanti ideal of female beauty, and which expectant mothers and children were encouraged to fondle in the hope that their children would be equally beautiful, were reasonably life-like. The life-like figurines of chiefs in Nigeria appear to have been archival in purpose. In the same way, commissioned portraits elsewhere easily serve the purpose of archives. When critics like Gombrich say that the African artists were incapable of realistic representation, they quite miss the point of African art. If they seek life-like representation, they should turn to secular art, the art which was produced for decorative purposes or the purposes of records, rather than moral art, the art whose inspiration is the intuition of a world force.

In examples of the mother suckling a child, the maternal expression of tenderness and solicitude is totally lacking in the mother's countenance. Instead, she tilts her head upwards, not downwards; she is erect and rigid, the unrelated seriousness on her face giving one the idea of occurring in a pattern and set-up of forces, already laid down for us. The Akans, like other African peoples, admitted no excuse for the abandonment of a child except as a religious obligation. The maternal care for a child was not a gift, not a matter of free personal relations, but a stipulation of ineluctable duty. Even the unnatural elongation of the mammary glands in such carvings sufficiently suggest a primeval force, a non-private, non-individual, choiceless arrangement.

Traditional African art was not literary or descriptive, employing conventionalised devices for effects like a kind of code-language. It was direct, magical, attempting a sort of plastic analogue of onomatopoeia, to evince and to evoke feelings which the subjects induced in one. It was a kind of para-ideography in wood, raffia, colour and stone. A similar effect is produced in African languages. Among the Zulus for example, the night from the depths of its darkness is almost supposed to be not blinding, but deafening. The expression for night and darkness is onomatopoeic of the particular sound that the night is supposed to utter. The name of night therefore seeks to promote the same feelings which night itself does. Among the Akans, too, there is a word, *munsum-munsum*, which evokes in one that sense of the sombre and the uncanny effluence which darkness and night in forest surroundings disengage around us. In sculpture, deformity was used on account of an already existing attitude to it. It was connected with evil and divine punishment. It was at least invested with a totally uncanny nature. The superlative achievement of African art probably lies in the control achieved over deformity and its associated feelings in their societies. Thus in the relevant works, there is near-vigour, but not vigour *à la* Japan, near-hideousness but not hideousness, near-distortion which is not complete, the complex of attributes which does not quite scarify, but leaves a ponderous aura of dark forces, of massive unreleased potency, of the unknown and the indeterminate, almost a hushed version of the ventriloquist ubiquity of the rattle-snake, the sense of mesmerised helplessness, still, cold, silent, enchantedly forlorn, and an aura of the numinous presence of primeval spirit. African art was testamental, except when it was secular.

It is, of course, dying out today. For example, the Ibibios of Nigeria carved skilful, reverent and sorrowful masks with which they covered the faces of their dead chiefs. They soon began to use 'fifth of November' caricatures. A number of reasons can be mentioned in explanation. First and foremost is its dislocation. The position of art in society has changed considerably in Africa with the loss of independence to Europe. It has lost its patronage. Furthermore, the poetic nature which produced the art is being undermined without balance by those attitudes which the impingement of science plus scepticism fosters. The pervasive sense of ultimacy about certain questions which forced one simply to utter a cry, is being lost in key positions in favour of the approach usually called scientific method. The art, which gave expression to that pervasive sense, now stands, like that sense, disgraced.

In the modern Europeanistic setting, art comes to be enjoyed for technical reasons, design, mixture of colours, or otherwise for its arbitrariness, as when a patch of paint is called 'the castle ruins'. Both types of reason equally represent the sloughing-off of art by society as a cement factor. Representation and photography in art are technical, not inspirational. Even the titillation under the skin which works of art deriving from the impressionistic tradition can produce belongs to representation. In Europe, testamental art perished with Goya.

Institutions and Theory

In the treatment of the Akan civilisation in a paradigmatic way, a number of features have emerged. The civilisation operated an essentialist doctrine of man, according to which man had an irreducible essence, which was constant and unchanging. This is a point on which one should expect similarity, if there is a unity in African cultures. This similarity is in fact there. The irreducible elements into which man is separated are of course not given the same names, and are not surrounded by a dogma which is on all points unvarying. It is, however, significant enough for unity that the type of separation should be the same, and that the dogma surrounding the elements, dogma relating to their origins and their dynamic roles, should in salient features be the same.

The ethics flowing from the essentialist conception are again substantially the same, both in the kind of justification and argument that they allow, and even also in the enunciation of rules, which tend towards communalism. Here again, of course, certain differences occur, but these details can be explained by reference to differences in local conditions. Thus, in an area where there are no pigs, to point at the absence of rules mentioning pigs would admittedly be a testimony to one's observation, but hardly to one's sagacity. Rules touching the membership of a family, rules governing responsibilities, the explanation of the responsibilities, the nature of society, and the explanation of its organisation; these are central points over which the identity of African cultures is established. To mention that some societies in Africa are quasi-monarchic and others nomadic is to miss a great deal. Should a monarchic or quasi-monarchic society lose its territory, its organisation, but not its beliefs, is bound to change. Indeed, sometimes, in order to put exactly the same beliefs into practice with different resources, one has to devise different institutions, and organise things differently. The exaggeration of the importance of institutional differences is a perversity that arises from the conception of method as being concerned with the immediately overt, and from the conception of explanation of all societies as the apotheosis of its quite static and inertia-ridden institutional framework as its essence, as that in terms of which, rather than simply by reference to which, striking features of the society must be explained. The effect of this is to treat the institutions as though they were self-mandated, and were only subject to an internal evolutionary principle. This, of course, is the wrong attitude to institutions. The approach becomes entirely insensitive to those silent forces which make even institutional changes easy or difficult, acceptable or unacceptable, legitimate or illegitimate. If one were to study the Church of England for example, it could never be sufficient to watch the behaviour of its members on Sundays when they go to church. True as it may be that people have gone to war for the right to genuflect, what they have fought for is not the simple anatomical posture that meets the eye. It presupposes a theology and a doctrine. To understand the Church of England, one has to take note of dogmatics. Ritual indeed enables one to express one's devotion in a satisfying way, but ritual is the result of concessions to realities of life, it represents a reaction between social facts and the religious mind. To suppose that ritual is the essence of religion is as quaint as regarding the signing of the register as the whole reality of the institution of marriage.

To understand a society as a dynamism, one has to look at the theory which underlies the institutions themselves. The explanation of the efficacy of an institution may sometimes be mechanistic, but the explanation of the choice of institutions, of their interrelation and subordination, cannot itself be mechanistic.

When one speaks of the unity of African cultures, one does not thereby imply any uniqueness. One does not necessarily wish to say that there is a certain minimal complex of significant elements which are common to African cultures and which are such that they have never been seen elsewhere before in the history of mankind. Such a claim would clearly be preposterous. After all, at the level of fundamentals there are only few alternatives which face mankind. A culture of man is either essentialist or not, lineages are either matrilinear or patrilinear or mixed. There are logical limits to versatility and creativity. Bearing in mind the fact that the world must have seen quite a few tribes in its time, one is not really surprised if at some time somewhere outside Africa, a people have arranged things in ways fundamentally identical to those in Africa. For the unity of African cultures, it is enough that the cultural complex should occur in sufficient areas of negro Africa. Unity does not imply uniqueness.

The similarity in the European domination of Africa, reacting with negro cultures similar among themselves, has led to urban cultures which are comparable. It has also led to substantially identical problems facing newly independent African countries. The question of what one does with political independence is a very genuine one. If a policy, deriving from the heritage of Africa, could be agreed pan-Africa-wise, then solutions validated within such a policy could be found and simply multiplied to the advantage of economy, effect, and natural unity. The variety of policies gives it today the aspect of multiple wounds. Agreement would draw the skin together, and give Africa a continental outlook.

CHAPTER 3

INDEPENDENCE
LOST AND REGAINED

The loss of independence: How to gain an Empire: Benefits of colonial-
ism—Evils of colonialism—Aspects of African enslavement—Sir John
Fielding's style—Some remarkable Africans—Africa's price for
revolution—Africa's development of Europe—The emergence of a new
class structure—The political inspiration of economics—Christianity
and individualism in Africa—The demand for independence: The
bearing of Russia—Liberal democracy—Designing institutions—
Political parties—Schisms and unity—One party states—Pressure
groups—The Settler problem—Extremism and Anti-colonialism—
Nationalism and Racialism—Soviet attitudes.

AFRICAN REGIONS LOST THEIR independence to European powers
through treaties, aggression, fraud or simple carelessness. The
treaties, aggressions and frauds were economically inspired.
In some cases, governors were commercial governors, and the
British Colonial Office at least showed some reluctance in
assuming administrative responsibility for the Gold Coast.
Wars were seldom for sheer conquest by European powers, but
were often deemed necessary to protect commerce. The British
campaigns against the Ashantis, for example, were not motivated
by desire for territorial aggrandisement, but by the importance
of peace to commercial activity.

To illustrate how some African areas lost their independence
through the opposite of straight dealing, one may cite the
dependency of Kenya. The Sultan of Zanzibar conceded the
administration of territories on the African mainland to Sir W.
Mackinnon, and a few other wealthy men of business, who
formed the Imperial East Africa Company. This company
was honoured with a Royal Charter in 1888.

Between 1887 and 1891, the energetic company agreed a
number of treaties with chiefs in the interior, who within the
laws of their own territories had no competence to surrender the
rights of their people in the land, and had not in any case, even
according to British law, surrendered them as this intention was

neither explicit nor implicit in their actions. Neither in East Africa nor in West Africa did the chiefs in their persons own the state lands. Ownership could therefore not be in their gift. They, however, abandoned their sovereign rights over their territories and peoples. When the Imperial East Africa Company surrendered its Charter, Kenya in 1895 became a British Protectorate. No new agreements were concluded with the people through their chiefs and under any law sovereignty over their territory and peoples should have reverted to chiefs. Kenya was, however, not immediately thought of as a possible area for settlers. When the railway to Uganda was being built it quickly became apparent that the surrounding lands were rich, and the climate mild, both suitable for European settlement. Suddenly, the idea of a white colony in the style of the ancient Greeks became attractive. Sir Charles Eliot, writing in 1905, thought that it was mere hypocrisy not to admit that white interests must be paramount and that the main object of British policy and legislation should be to found a white colony. Since 1902, Britain had been making grants, quite *ultra vires*, of land to European syndicates and individuals. By 1921, even the judiciary had formed the opinion that all African rights in the land had disappeared, by what magic one can hardly form a firm and distinct idea. A decision of the Kenya High Court made the Africans out as having become tenants at will of the Crown. It is hardly surprising therefore that Empire Loyalists should feel sore at what in their naïve enthusiasm they conceive to be the throwing away of British land to natives at independence. The granting of independence becomes to them a gesture of largesse as impudent and idiotic as it is treasonable. The *bizarrerie* of the British claim did not quite escape Lord Buckmaster, once a Lord Chancellor, who said in the House of Lords: 'How the Crown asserted and obtained the rights of ownership over the whole soil is due to a series of legal fictions which is not always easy to follow.' (Parliamentary Debates, House of Lords, vol. 61, no. 44, p. 402.)

As to treaties, there is the case of the sad Ewe chief who had signed himself and his people under the protection of Queen Victoria. For certain reasons, Britain decided to transfer this section of the Ewes to the Germans. The Ewe chief, heavy of heart, told the British factor there that it was quite freely that he had transferred himself and his people to Queen Victoria. If Her Britannic Majesty was now tired of them he would have thought that they should be transferred to themselves. He had not asked for the Germans, and was very devoted to the Queen. These, of course, were high matters of state and who could allow the Ewe sentimentality to impede high-minded politic decisions? The transference to the Germans was duly made.

Through the carelessness of everybody and the admirable hypocrisy of King Leopold, the Congo became his private estate.

And as for the poor Portuguese, the will of God, set down for everyone to read in a papal Bull, encumbered them with an Eastern hemisphere which heresy has reduced to Angola, Mozambique, and a few other minor remnants.

However it came about, the loss of independence became a ubiquitous fact in Africa. It must be admitted that this has brought items into Africa which, absolutely speaking, must be accounted to be of benefit to the continent. The abolition of the slave trade is one such item. The opposition of Africans to its abolition was appreciable, and there is a story of a chief in the Niger delta, who when exhorted to sell elephant tusks instead of men replied with more wit than humanity that it was far easier to catch a man than an elephant. By abolishing the slave trade, however, a move in which Britain stands honoured for her initiative, a halt was put to the depopulation of Africa by that means. Africa has even now not fully recovered in population terms from the drain. Legitimate commerce was increased.

Formal schools were introduced in non-Moslem areas, and in Moslem areas they were augmented and broadened. Scientific health services were introduced, and the backbones of malaria and a host of debilitating diseases were broken. Roads were built to replace the bush paths which linked the countless villages festering on the African soil. Peace was assured. All these are notable gains from the despair at the loss of independence, and they genuinely mark an improvement in Africa.

But these blessed items were not introduced in a simple way. Colonialism in Africa has brought its own miseries. The slave trade in the vicious form that it took was created by Europe. It is said that of Europeans, Alonzo Gonzales, the Portuguese, was the first man to point out Africans to his countrymen as articles of commerce—in 1434. In 1440, having kidnapped twelve Africans, he put a woman among them on the shore in the hope that her people would come forward to redeem her. Next day, some hundred and fifty appeared. The Portuguese did not feel venturesome on that day, and they were handsomely treated to a volley of stones. The Portuguese were in turn followed by the Spaniards, the Dutch, the French, and the English.

Soon, Africans began to desert the coast, and when it became more difficult to catch them, the Portuguese, again first in Europe, decided to build forts and castles. They showed all the marks of liberalism and friendship. They brought presents, a peaceful deportment and messages from their king. In 1481, they built their famous castle at Elmina, San Diego d'Elmina. The castle stands to this day. In order that a steady supply of slaves should be maintained by the chiefs who let themselves be quickly seduced, new offences were created and old ones sophisticated. Offenders of the first degree forfeited their own freedom. Offenders of the second degree also forfeited the freedom of the male part of their family. Offenders of the third degree involved the female part as well. And the accursed offenders of the fourth degree committed all their relations as far as could be traced. Though the corruption and barbarism of the coastal Africans was great, they could not sell their own children. The Europeans argued in the seventeenth and eighteenth centuries that if the Africans had the right to sell their own children the Europeans certainly had the right to buy them. This argument arose from a misunderstanding of an African word which could be used to refer to one's son, one's servant, or anyone of a lower status than oneself. Roemer, the Dane, writing in 1749, refuted the argument in point of fact.

All along, there had been agitations in Europe for the abolition of the slave trade. Bartholomew de las Casas, the

Bishop of Chiapa, went to Spanish America and was greatly perturbed by the cruelty which slavery incited in the Spanish temperament. He came back to Spain and entered a public remonstrance before the king. The king greatly admired his speech, but though the bishop had threatened him with the displeasure of Heaven for allowing cruelties which he had the power to stop, the certainty of economic gain proved stronger than anxieties concerning the Day of Judgment. In the seventeenth century, Morgan Godwyn, an English clergyman, became noted for his condemnation of slavery. In the middle of the eighteenth century John Woolman and Anthony Benezet applied themselves with that degree of earnestness which one associates with Quakers to the move to abolish slavery. The former walked around North America remonstrating against the holding of others in involuntary subjection by Quakers, and the latter established a free school at Philadelphia for the education of negroes.

In 1754, the religious Society of Friends solemnly declared that 'to live in ease and plenty by the toil of those whom fraud and violence had put into their power, was neither consistent with Christianity nor common justice'. This, of course, was a slightly misleading attestation, for it might have given the impression that Friends mixed their own horror of plenty and ease with the quite distinct evil which slavery was. Many of the Society, with that fresh directness of Quakers which eschewed sophistry, slashed away the chains of their slaves. It is said that they high-mindedly considered that 'to possess a little in an honourable way, was better than to possess much through the medium of injustice'. Armed with this philosophical maxim, they settled down to a period of pious poverty. Those who were half-hearted about this were threatened with expulsion from the Society. Many of the slaves, at a loss what to do with their new-won freedom in a strange land, returned to former owners as hired servants. It was considered that the productivity of the freed slaves grew with their new status. The Quakers were not slow to draw an inference concerning the relation of prosperity to virtue.

With this example to draw upon, members of the Roman

Catholic Church, Presbyterians, and the Church of England began to free their slaves in significant numbers. This movement did not start without some difficulty. At a Synod in Pennsylvania, when Presbyterians discussed the possibility of invoking the curse of Heaven on recalcitrant owners of slaves, the bid to do this was duly defeated by a democratic majority of one. The opposition was actuated, not by any wickedness of heart, but by a peace-loving dislike of threats and force on any matters, including property.

In Britain, the Quakers were equally active, and of all religious fellowships they were at this time the most militant. Somehow, however, many of them seem to have gained the impression that there were no slaves in Britain. Their efforts took the form of petitions to Parliament, seeking Parliament's interference in what they called the iniquitous African trade. A few of them formed the hypothesis that these petitions proved ineffectual because 'the unsupported efforts of piety, morality and justice' were weak 'against interest, violence and oppression'. Thomas Clarkson, who wrote a prize-winning essay at Cambridge, acknowledged with self-confessed blushings that the latter forces were 'too strongly countenanced by the legislative authority of a country, the basis of whose government is liberty'.

Of course, Granville Sharpe had shown interest in abolition earlier on, in 1766. It was during litigation concerning his activities that Chief Justice Holt had delivered it as his opinion that whoever set his foot on English soil by that very act made himself a free man. In 1720, Talbot and Hardwicke, as slippery a brace of lawyers as could be found, had suggested that the physical act of a slave coming into Britain did not confer the formal status of freedom on him, and he could be deported to the plantations where he belonged. In 1749, when Hardwicke had a chance to back his opinion with some authority, he ruled that a runaway slave could be recovered. Indeed, His Majesty's officials sometimes more than lent a hand in the recovery of delinquent slaves. Latimer claims that the postmaster-general of Bristol had been employed to recapture a slave in hiding in Bristol.

Another wicked ruse to defraud slave-owners of their

property was duly defeated. Christians, not unreasonably, felt that any slave who had received the sacrament of baptism must surely be free instantaneously, as through baptism he became a child of God, a member of Christ and an inheritor of the Kingdom of Heaven. Lawyers once again patiently explained that though the baptismal rite did confer freedom, unfortunately it only touched the soul, ushering the African soul from the primeval darkness in which it wallowed, into the beatific light and glory of God. Baptism, a purely spiritual undertaking, could not be deemed to affect the material condition of slaves.

Struck by the uncertainty of the future and the unpleasantness of the present, runaway slaves dived into an underground of misery and poverty, and quite often appeared at the Old Bailey on charges of petty theft. Sometimes they were treated with considerable sympathy, sometimes they met with the full incorruptibility of the law.

In 1780, when one of them had been accused of being a Gordon rioter, Sir John Fielding, bursting with irritation, at first gently protested against the shipment of slaves to Britain, deeming it an unfairness that they should have been 'instructed in the necessary qualifications of a domestic servant at a vast expense' merely to be brought afterwards to England 'as cheap servants without the right to wages'. But warming to his subject he went on:

'They no sooner arrive here than they put themselves on a footing with other servants, become intoxicated with liberty, grow refractory, and either by persuasion of others or from their own inclinations, begin to expect wages according to their own opinion of their merits; and as there are already a great number of black men and women who have made themselves so troublesome and dangerous to the families who have brought them over to get themselves discharged, these enter into societies and make it their business to corrupt and dissatisfy the mind of every black servant that comes to England; first by getting them christened or married, which, they inform them, makes them free . . . though it has not been decided otherwise by the judges. However, it so far answers their purpose that it gets the mob on their side and makes it not only difficult but dangerous . . . to recover possession of them, when once they are spirited away, and indeed, it is the less evil of the two to let them go about their business, for there is great reason that those blacks who have been sent back to the plantations have been the occasion of those . . . recent insurrections in the West Indies. It is a species of inhumanity to the blacks themselves to bring them to a free country.'

Sir John had a fine style.

The Reverend James Ramsay perused colonial codes of law, hopelessly seeking clauses by means of which the grievances of slaves might be redressed. He published a treatise called *An Essay on the treatment and Conversion of African Slaves in the British Sugar Colonies*. This treatise was published at the expense of forfeiting friendships in the West Indies, hazarding loss of private property, and the ill-will and annoyance of numerous individuals at home. Two replies were published in eight months. The first was called *Cursory Remarks on Mr Ramsay's Essay*, and charged him alternatively with exaggeration or falsehood. The *Cursory Remarks* were adjudged by Ramsay's friends to be a creditable effort at composition, but devoid of truth. They were a virulent attack on Ramsay, full of insinuations a bit disturbing about a man of God.

The other reply, *The Apology for Negro Slavery*, asserted that people were never kidnapped on the west coast of Africa, that the treatment of slaves was of the very mildest nature, living as they did in the most comfortable and happy manner imaginable. One can be forgiven for suspecting that both the perception and the imagination of the author were considerably blunted. Still, he proposed as regulations that the kidnapping of people into slavery from Africa should become felonious, likewise the premeditated murder of a slave in transit. In 1781, 132 Africans bound for the American plantations were jettisoned into the sea alive in order to defraud underwriters. It was also suggested that when slaves arrived in the Colonies land should be appointed to them according to their number, that they should not work on Sundays or other holidays, that overtime or night work out of crop be banned, that a limited number of stripes be awarded, a suit of clothes a year, and finally that old and infirm slaves be properly cared for.

Does one see here intimations of a Socialist Revolution?

Of course, the abolitionists were realist enough to devise economic arguments. Of all the things that could be clearly shown, they considered it the most clearly shown that '. . . an inexhaustible mine of wealth is neglected in Africa, for the prosecution of this impious traffic; that, if proper measures were taken, the revenue of this country might be greatly improved, its naval strength increased, its colonies in a more flourishing situation, the planters richer, and a trade, which is now a source of blood and desolation, converted into one which might be prosecuted with advantage and honour.'

By bringing humanitarian works to the frontiers of economic treaties, the abolitionists eventually won. When there were enough slaves across the Atlantic for agricultural and domestic purposes Britain flaunted the light by banning the trade. When there was the assurance that slave industries across the Atlantic would be under-employed, the status of slavery was again abolished by Britain. Of course, there is no necessary connection here, but the fact would not have escaped one that the Africans sent across could not return to Africa in sufficient numbers to threaten the labour market. And the Adam Smith kind of argument according to which forced labour was unproductive was already widely believed. To the honour of Britain, it carried out and enforced the dual abolition in the teeth of the opposition.

In South Africa, the Dutch colonists had settled to a destruction of their Hottentots for pleasure. Andrew Sparman, a Physics Professor at Stockholm and Fellow of the Royal Academy of Sciences, was one of those who expressed their shock, after a visit in 1785.

In Holland, the debate assumed an academic flavour, as very few Africans came to that country. The Dutch contented themselves with the transatlantic trade. Debate more often centred on the mental and moral qualities of the African than on his social status. All the same there was an African student at the University of Leiden, Jacobus Eliza Capitein from the Gold Coast, who in 1738 wrote a treatise in which he argued that slavery was not incompatible with Christianity and could indeed be its instrument. He practically thanked Europe for the slave trade, but for which he would not be studying at Leiden, lionised for his skill at Latin and divinity. He returned to the

Gold Coast in 1742 and became a predicant at the Castle of San George d'Elmina, then in Dutch hands. In 1745, he wrote a letter to the Elders of the Dutch West Indies Company in Holland begging to be allowed to marry an African woman who seemed very modest and beautiful, lest the Evil One should triumph over him. He was prepared to send her to Holland for inspection and further Christian education.

In France, there were a number of publications stating both sides of the case in the proper manner including an abolitionist treatise under the pseudonym of Raynal and translated into English in 1792. The French Assembly heard a number of addresses in favour of Africans and persons of mixed blood by Henri Gregoire, Constitutional Bishop of Blois, including a moving one in 1789. He wrote comparative studies of ancient and modern slavery, and in 1808 published a book on the intellectual and moral faculties of the negroes and their achievements in letters and science. He appended short biographical notices on fifteen of them.

Of course replies were forthcoming, and F. R. de Tussac in particular published an outcry of the colonists against Gregoire, and purported to refute the slanderous accusations suffered by them. He followed this up sixteen years later, in 1826, with a treatise on the nobility of the skin. This condemned the pro-Negro philosophers.

Abolition, however, was of the nature of a revolution and this cannot fail to enhance its virtue. J. H. van Eurie, writing in New York in 1861 in *Negroes and Negro Slavery*, said,

'The Southern planter, with a consciousness of superiority that would be ashamed to resort to fiction or imposition of any kind, takes off his coat and works in the same field and at the same labours as his slave. The thought of the latter contesting his superiority never once enters his mind. As said by a sound statesman and gallant soldier of the South, "we no more think of a negro insurrection, than we do of a rebellion of our cows and horses". The planter rules as naturally as the negro obeys instinctively; the relation between them is natural, harmonious, and necessary, and their interests being indivisible, there can be no cause or motive, either for the abuse of power on the part of the master, or of rebellion on the part of the servant.'

Today, the South appears to have meant its words.

The period of slavery threw up a number of notable Africans in Europe and America. Records of some of them have survived. Of the European ones, one may mention Attobah Coguano, Ignatius Sancho, Gustavus Vassa, and Anton Wilhelm Amo. Capitein has already been mentioned. Attobah Coguano was born in Ajumako in Ghana, and, while still a boy, was kidnapped with twenty others of both sexes by Europeans brandishing pistols and sabres. In his autobiography, which was published in English and translated into French, he told how he and his companions were confined and heard nothing but the clanging of chains, the sound of the whip, and the cries of fellow prisoners. Of his departure, the invocation of Heaven and the tear-baths, he says that 'this spectacle, calculated to move the hearts of monsters, does not that of human life; and believe me, my friend, that a victory gained over possible immorality and pride is more deserving of a *Te Deum* than that which is obtained in the field of ambition and carnage'.

In Grenada, where they were taken, they were severely beaten because, instead of working on Sundays, they indolently went to church. (Of course, the opinions of Africans on Sunday had not been praised before. In West Africa, for instance, there was a Governor who had given Africans instruction in the scriptures; he called them together one day and asked them what they knew of God. God, one of them said, was much loved among them because he had created two things: one was Sunday, on which one did not work, and the other was sleep, during which one did not work. In Grenada, when the African workers sucked sugar-cane, their masters brilliantly went to the root of the trouble, and teeth were broken.) Eventually, however, Lord Hoth secured Coguano's freedom, and brought him over to England. In 1788, he was in the service of Cosway, who was then the first painter to the Prince of Wales. Coguano lived in London and married an English woman. Piatoli, a friend of his, spoke highly of him, and singled out his piety, mildness of character, modesty, integrity, and talents for extensive praise.

Ignatius Sancho was born on a slave-ship which was taking his parents away into slavery. It was at Carthagena that he was given the name Ignatius. John Lok, who sailed for the West Coast of Africa in 1554 and brought back with his cargo 'certaine blacke slaves whereof some were tall and strong men', had said that the Africans found English food and the English way of life tolerable enough, though 'the colde and moyst aire doth somewhat offend them'. Ignatius' mother was greatly offended by the change of climate, and she quietly died away. Ignatius' father killed himself, while, one supposes, the balance of his mind was disturbed. Ignatius, now at the ripe age of two, was brought to England, and presented to three sisters, all of them young ladies, who lived at Greenwich. His character, as he grew up, became so picturesque and wise that he was given the surname Sancho. The Duke of Montague, out riding for some reason, saw Sancho in tears, stopped, questioned him, took a fancy to him, and lent him books. The Duke also advised on his education. With the Duke dead, Sancho plunged into difficulties, and squirmed in them, until the Duchess in pity employed him as butler. She left him seventy pounds in cash, and an annuity of thirty pounds. Again, he fell into bad ways, until at length he was engaged in the service of a respectable family. His conduct improved, and he married a lady born in the West Indies. He settled down to raising a family with characteristic single-mindedness, and in a short time had rather a large one to his name.

He gained public esteem by his domestic virtues, though he developed gout in 1773. The Duchess of Kent was a friend, and she received from Sancho numerous letters in which advice and exhortation were freely given. For some reason, he was markedly fond of quoting from Deuteronomy. He published his reflections on the slave trade, and the enslavement of Africans. His book was translated into French. He died in 1780, and a posthumous edition of his collected letters came out.

Gustavus Vassa was born Olandoh Equiano to a vassal of the King of Benin in Nigeria. Kidnapped with his sister, he was sold to the Christians and sent to Virginia. There, he was bought by a Captain M. H. Pascal, who brought him over to England, bestowed the name Vassa on him, and deposited him in Guernsey. Vassa took part in the expedition against Louisbourg under Admiral Boschaven in 1758. He sailed in the same ship as General Wolfe, to whose affability he constantly testified. He himself became a Christian in 1759.

In 1779, the following letter was addressed to the Bishop of London.

My Lord

I have resided near seven years on the coast of Africa, for most part of the time as commanding officer. From the knowledge I have of the country and its inhabitants, I am inclined to think that the within plan will be attended with great success, if countenanced by your Lordship. I beg leave further to represent to your Lordship that the like attempts, when encouraged by other governments, have met with uncommon success, and at this very time I know a very respectable character, a black priest at Cape Coast Castle. I know the within named Gustavus Vassa, and I believe him a moral man. I have the honour to be,

My Lord,
Your Lordship's
Humble and Obedient Servant,
Matt. Macnamara.

His Lordship, however, declined what was desired, to ordain Vassa. Instead, he received a Royal Commission as Commissary for Provisions and Stores for the Black Poor of Sierra Leone. In the same year, 1787, he married a daughter of James and Ann Cullen, who lived in Ely. He was mentioned in the *Gentleman's Magazine* for August 1792 and in the *Literary and Biographical Magazine* for May 1792.

Anton Wilhelm Amo was born near Axim about the year 1700. His parents had been converted to Christianity of the species of the Dutch Reformed Church. He himself was sent to Holland through the instrumentality of Johannes van der Star, a preacher in the Gold Coast, to study more of the Christian principles, free from the seductions of his heathen compatriots, in order to come back as a priest and teacher. The Dutch West Indies Company, who were responsible both for the Dutch trade in Ghana and the Dutch missionary effort, were reluctant to bear the expenses, once Amo was in Holland; and they were unable to find anyone there who would take him immediately. It happened, however, that the Duke of Brunswick, Anton Ulric, sloughing off the Augsburg Confession, had published Fifty Reasons why one should become a Roman Catholic. Convinced by his own fifty reasons, he duly became one. Amo lived in his house at Wolfenbüttel until he entered the University of Halle, and in 1729 publicly defended his dissertation, *De Jure Maurorum in Europa*, a rather patriotic, if racialistic subject. He argued, basing himself on history and law, that African kings had in ancient times been vassals of the Roman Empire, and that each of them had held a royal patent, which Justinian too had granted; but they had to fetch it from Rome themselves. He went on to say that through this connection with the Romans the Africans had inherited laws such that their purchase and enslavement by European Christians was not right. Amo was attempting to minimise relevant differences between the African civilisation and the Christian, which Christians used as a justification for slavery. He moved on to Wittenberg and, while Kant was still a boy, became a Master of Philosophy there. In 1734, he defended a work in which he argued that sensation was not a mental faculty. Some of his conclusions were startling for his time. He held that if ideas of perception were in the mind at all, they could only be there by way of mode, because of the way in which empiricists conceived ideas. Since this was impossible he concluded that there were no such things in the mind. Any philosophy that made mind both active and passive involved for him a self-contradiction. And the mode of the presence of ideas of sensation in the human mind is truly a constant embarrassment for empiricist philosophers. Amo was a rationalist philosopher after Leibnitz, whom as a boy he had met at the Duke of Brunswick's. His performance was greatly praised. And the Chairman and Faculty members described him as a most noble and most renowned man from Africa, extraordinarily honest, diligent, and so erudite that he stood above his mates. In 1738, he produced his *magnum opus*, a book on logic, theory of knowledge and metaphysics.

He was well liked and well respected, and had led a procession at the visit of Frederick of Prussia to Halle in 1733. The Emperor was so pleased with the turn-out that he made a present of buckets of Rhine wine. He defied a ban by Frederick of Prussia on Wolff and his ideas, and lectured in Halle on the political thought of Wolff. In 1739 he moved to Jena, where he taught. In all, therefore, Amo taught at the Universities of Wittenberg, Halle and Jena. He took a sentence from Epictetus as his motto: 'He that accommodates himself to necessity is a wise man, and he has an inkling of things divine.' He wrote this down, as he said, to the perpetual memory of himself. He knew Hebrew, Greek, Latin, Dutch, French and German. If he had taken the trouble to learn English more about him would be known today. His success in Germany was probably symbolised in his nomination as a Counsellor of the Court of Berlin. He returned to Ghana some time after 1743 and died of boredom.

It was something, however, that these men could come by any education then. Fewer bars are placed today on Africans wanting to study in Europe than then. In 1731, for example, the Lord Mayor and Aldermen of London passed an ordinance forbidding the teaching of trades to negroes. When they had some education, the fruits of this were not always admired. Of the passion for freedom of Francis Barber, servant of Doctor Johnson, Boswell says 'with all deference, that, in suchwise, he discovered a zeal without discretion'. He also felt aggrieved by the attempts being made to 'abolish so very necessary and important a branch of commercial interest'.

Some of the Africans grew content with being kept in Britain as slaves, at a time when Scotsmen were sold as slaves. The eighteenth and nineteenth centuries present innumerable cases of wives being publicly sold in London by their husbands. *The Times* of July 19th, 1797, has the following passage:

'By some mistake in our report of the Smithfield Market we had not learned the average price for wives for the last week ... the increasing value of the fair sex is esteemed by several eminent writers as a certain criterion of increasing civilisation. Smithfield has, on this ground, strong pretensions of refined improvement, as the price of wives has risen in that market from half-a-guinea to three guineas-and-a-half.'

Of all the tragedies that the world has seen, it is the persecution of the Jews which comes nearest to the enslavement of Africa.

The slave trade is Africa's price for the intellectual revolution which the contact with Europe has meant to her.

Africa's price continues to be paid in the twentieth century, if in a somewhat attenuated form. It was the opinion of Lord Burnham near the beginning of the century that it would not have been possible to carry on the industries of Europe without the gold from South Africa. He might have mentioned that Africa is the one factor that has had the most crucial significance for Europe. The slave trade provided the cheapest imaginable labour; gold was obtained either from mines or from absurdly inequitable trade. The formation of capital which made the industrial revolution possible was guaranteed by Africa. In this century too, Europe has continued to depend directly on mineral substances that it has taken from Africa, including gold, manganese, uranium, bauxite, tin, oil, iron. Diamonds are almost limitless.

The copper mines of Katanga helped greatly in deciding the first world war. Hundreds of tons of copper were shipped from there to Britain, and other countries, and used in the munitions and armament industry. It is said that at the same time the Germans were raking in saucepans and chamber pots for the purpose. The efficiency of British aeroplanes too was greatly increased at the discovery, during the war, of manganese in the Gold Coast. It also ensured a continuous supply of chlorine gas.

Europe also obtained vegetable substances including rubber, fibres, coffee, sugar, fats, fruits, cotton.

All the mines of Africa, and all the farms of Africa, both those of Africans and those of others, have been worked with African labour. Sometimes the labour has been free, sometimes it has been involuntary.

It is said that forced labour is prejudicial to its local economy because it reduces productivity. It is thought to do this because workers lose the interest which they might have had, a considerable proportion of energy is wasted both by the stubborn dilatoriness of the workers and through the more vigorous supervision required. Application becomes neither conscientious nor continuous. There springs a sense of alienation from work which, if unchecked, could become firm. In many areas in Africa, even with the arrival of independence, workers were to be heard explaining or recommending dilatoriness by saying that one did not perform the white man's task with greed.

But forced labour is perhaps not as prejudicial to the local economy in a socialistic framework as it is in a capitalistic one, because in the former it has a chance of tincture with idealism, whereas in the latter it can only be urged with shibboleths about the dignity of the labour of others. That a state has some right to the services of its citizens is indeed beyond argument, but it is necessary that such services should be geared directly to the communal purpose and that all those who are able to contribute to it should do so. The best method of guaranteeing this is through taxation except for amenities at a very parochial level.

Forced labour has been exacted in Africa by all her colonial powers. To build the Midland Railway in what was the French Cameroons, men were forced to work for seven months in the year without pay. The authorities confessed that the associated deaths were at the rate of eighty per thousand, and admitted that every six thousand persons had the attention of one doctor.

In Kenya, a magistrate sentenced a number of Africans for refusing to comply with an order to compulsory labour on the railway. The Kenya Supreme Court, however, quashed the conviction (in 1925).

Labour was procured for the building of railways in Portuguese and Belgian territories in Africa in the same way.

The British refused to permit forced labour for private profit in Africa, though in 1925 a request was made to the Governor of Southern Rhodesia for precisely that. It was condemned by Lord Cromer as being synonymous with slavery. It is still practised in South Africa, Mozambique, Angola, and Spanish Africa with epic savagery.

The League of Nations Mandate for Africa did indeed allow compulsory labour limited to essential public services, but even then it stipulated adequate remuneration. But the French, with their tidy ratiocinative minds, imposed a fiscal labour levy, explaining that this was commutable for money payment in tax—a rather otiose explanation in an area where wages were then almost non-existent. There were mainly four means of forceful persuasion when Africans proved a little intractable. They were deprived of their land, vagrancy laws were enacted, direct taxes were imposed, and the communalistic conscience was invoked.

At the very parochial level, these methods of persuasion led to little enough friction because they appealed among other things to the forces of the African society as touching communalism, for instance. In such accidental ways, the loss of independence acquired preservative aspects. As regards the cultures of Africa, the mass that has survived confirms the view that metropolitan powers have not sought in any systematic way to obliterate the African soul. The small percentage of westernised Africans, who were only administratively effective in their own countries, is testimony thereto. If they had also become cultural or moral leaders, the impact of colonialism would have been complete.

Even so, it has blunted the mettle of the peoples, through gobbling up their purposefulness. It has raised in them the feeling that they have been but appendages, incidental merely to other men's business. This is not to say, however, that colonialism has destroyed the initiative of the peoples. The purposefulness and single-mindedness with which independence has been pursued would seem to point enough at initiative. In fact, it is precisely through making the indigenous cultures irrelevant, through passing them by, that they have been contained within themselves with their potential of initiative. Indirect rule through chiefs was one of the gravest mistakes of colonialism from its own point of view, for it was conservative of indigenous culture, and so perpetuating of the alienation between them and the metropolitan cultures, against which the indigenous ones are firmly posed with the attainment of independence. The West Indies, where the acculturation into Europe has gone very far, will by contrast find very little to pose against the European cultures now or at independence. The West Indies are Western and might do well to accelerate the process of westernisation as the only really practical alternative given to them.

If one takes one of the pervasive aspects of societies, class structure, one finds that the type of role that class differences play in the West Indies is substantially parallel to the role in the West. The class structure is horizontal, not vertical, as in Africa. In the West Indies, one finds Europeans and Americans who own plantations, persons of mixed African-European or Indian-European descent, and persons of African descent or Indian descent. The stratification of the society is in that sequence. The stratification in terms of descent parallels the stratification in terms of wealth. The introduction of electoral politics has naturally strengthened the hands of the lowest strata, and the old criteria of stratification are yielding to compromise here and there. It appears that the tendency in the West Indies is for the middle class and the top strata of the working class to vote together, thus linking class with power. In traditional Africa, class did not, of course, connect itself with power. Power offices involved specialisms, and they were electorally filled on occasion in a way transcending class susceptibilities. Distinction in wisdom and the arts required were usually considered necessary for the holding of specialist offices, just as in the growing tendency in modernistic societies.

Side by side with the traditional class structure, during the loss of independence new elements of a class kind were introduced, certainly, and in these class was linked with administrative power. But this link was gravely debilitated by the rise of mass popular parties and movements. In the disappearance of a practically hereditary class unconnected with special skills, but wallowing in power, the new African countries have one of the marks of the true nationhood. Classes here are co-operative, not antagonistic as in the Marxian account. In spirit, the new African countries are nearer the welfare type of society than the West. They always have been, to the best of their means.

Apart from the political effects involved in the setting aside of the traditional life of the peoples, and the introduction of new types of social differentiation that the period of the loss of independence has seen, one might cite the new kind and scale of economic activity introduced with its constructive and its destructive powers, the new education together with its new religion and morality, changes in art and music and literature, in dress and food, changes in the techniques and the system of government and the political understructure of this system. The economic changes have had both a political and a social effect. They have turned the dependent countries into raw-material economies, and at the same time into market economies, with the unsatisfactory result that these countries without being industrialised accustomed themselves to the pleasures which industrialisation brings with it. They have sold their produce at the very low price which raw materials fetch, and relatively squandered their income on finished products at prices inflated by metropolitan wage-packets, marketing techniques and the maximisation of profits dogma. Whereas in the metropolitan countries, prices are said to be determined by wages and the amount of money floating around more than by demand, in the dependent countries they are not so arrived at. Many goods cost about the same in dependent and metropolitan countries. even though wages in dependent countries are far less than in metropolitan countries, and even though the amount of money floating around is much, much less. Though, nominally, the currency may be the same, the purchasing power is obviously not to be compared. It is evident that economic facts are not purely economic, but are also strongly nationalistic. If one spoke purely economically, then there would be a great deal to say for metropolitan countries setting up their factories in dependent countries and exporting their skilled labour thither. The saving in pay to unskilled labour, which is always very considerable, would be appreciable. And surpluses which could not be sold in dependent countries might be sold in the metropolitan countries themselves, who would have been manufacturing for home consumption. This course could naturally never be done because it would lead to unemployment at home, and it might also mean a reduction in the potential home market. But the outcry that might be raised in metropolitan countries could equally well be raised by dependent countries on their own behalf. The conflict of interest involved is irreducible as long as the dependent countries are not incorporated in the metropolitan territory, but retain their subject status.

The introduction of regular wages, and their payment to individuals instead of families, is another economic arrangement whose effect on the traditional society has been fundamental. It has given the individual a sense of private power. The levying of taxes on his head which were paid by him, his personal accountability for debts which he incurred and his personal expiation, under the metropolitan jurisdiction, of all crimes which he committed, the conversion of individuals instead of families to Christianity, with the Christian New Testament, but not Old Testament teaching, of the exclusive accountability of the individual conscience to God, together increased his sense of atomism. He was thus encouraged to think and act more on an atomistic, and less on a communalistic, basis.

The new Christian religion, with its morality founded on divine command, has not initiated much change except largely among recipients of Western education. The religious earnestness of those who have not received this education has been preserved in or outside the Christian Churches. With those who have received such education, however, it has tended on occasion to be ritualistic, nearly as much so as it often is in the metropolitan countries themselves. Church-going has sometimes been an exercise not of devout worship, but of social occasion, though, of course, there are also in large numbers deeply committed and devout Christians.

The Christian morality is, ideally, bound first and foremost by the moral usages laid down in the Gospels, especially in the Sermon on the Mount; and, if one is sufficiently impressed by the interpretations and additions found in the Epistles, one accepts them too. Thirdly, one also accepts the moral attitudes implicit in the Gospels themselves. In a society into which Christianity is introduced, there already exists a moral plenum, not a vacuum. Conceivably, there will be questions on which the Gospels are none too explicit, and imply no very clear direction. Some of these questions will already be decided by the extra-religious morality. This perhaps is what makes Christians in dependent territories so markedly tolerant of polygamy, for example. A morality can at no time be held to be a completely closed system, even when it is rationalistic. At any point, it still leaves certain choices and decisions open when uncharacteristic predicaments arise. To pursue the example of polygamy, the Gospels are certainly not very instructive on it, and though some people point out that if God had desired polygamy, He would have provided Adam with more than Eve, the legitimacy of this inference cannot be strongly felt. Some, too, point out that Jesus explained marriage to be a union in which man and woman became one flesh. Though one can see how one man may at once be one flesh with a multiplicity of women, the women themselves cannot between them be said in the same sense to be one flesh. But even this argument is not very luminous. One remembers that, historically at least, monogamy was a recommendation of the Council of Trent under Leo XIII. The findings of Catholic lions like St Thomas, Alexander of Hales, St Bonaventure, and Duns Scotus in favour of monogamy was repudiated by Durandus of Pourcain, Tostatus, Cajetan. Nor did either Luther or Melanchthon confess to any obligation to monogamy. Monogamy is probably an instance of extra-religious morality.

The practice of religion is of course not the whole of life. It is needful that religion should not be allowed to make undue havoc of areas of life adjacent and complementary to it, patterns of life which belong to the political economy. Fortunately, religious differences have not constituted themselves today into destructive forces in Africa. In the religious rivalries in Africa, one might however remember that there have been countless debates on Christianity and Islam, and some of the verdicts will be meaningless to Africa. It is well-known that the motives and the forces which settle religious reformations do not always flow from the nature of God, and an introduced religion depends for the depth of its success on the extent to which it can overcome or accommodate elements in the society into which it is introduced. Islam has possibly done more of the latter than Christianity in Africa.

The period of the loss of independence has, of course, brought into Africa the benefits of systematic education, an enrichment of the religious and the moral life, an enrichment of art, music, literature, dress, food. It has also equipped Africa with techniques of government irreplaceable in the management of effective contemporary states.

The demand of Africa for political independence became most organised in the twentieth century. But even in the nineteenth century, there had been conflicts of a political nature centring largely on the alienation of land. Stocktaking of the effect of Europe on Africa was already in progress, and, naturally, gloomy and cheerful pictures were painted. In the twentieth century, the turn that the resistance to independence demands took made it tactical to emphasise the gloomy aspects of colonialism. And they were indeed serious for Africa. The end of the second world war is a convenient dating-point for the political future of Africa. One must admit without reservation that the Africans who came to Europe and America for their education turned up a number of African patriots. Africans who had been in Europe had already pointed at the discrepancy between declarations concerning liberty and democracy on the one hand, and on the other the realities of colonialism. This was irritating. And Africans declared that they preferred self-government with danger to servitude in tranquillity. Britain, quick off the mark, started making arrangements for independence, helpfully encouraged by African political movements. And the prospects of Africans seeing pragmatic sincerity and seriousness in the terminology of politics truly shone.

In 1956, when the Gold Coast, led by the Convention Peoples' Party, was already in view of independence, French political leaders accused Britain and the Soviet Union of sabotaging the French Empire, actuated by envy. Britain and France, the European countries with most territorial commitments in Africa, have now greatly dispossessed themselves in that continent. But this process has been accompanied by debates, which are at their most excruciating today. There are certain elements involved in the granting of independence which have lain outside the public debate.

The fact of Russia, to take an instance, cannot be overlooked, but it must be seen rightly. Though Russia encouraged tendencies towards political movements, it would not have gone to war over them any more than it would now. Of course, to do so would be idiotic, unless Russia could be certain of winning with economy. A decade ago, Russia was not certain of winning at all, and today, is not certain of winning with economy. However much Russia desires the political freedom of African territories, it is obvious that there is nothing in the situation of sufficient urgency and interest to Russia to move her into forcing a showdown. The effect of Russia on the colonial question is therefore not one of offering a direct threat to Europe.

It was suspected in the West that the political régime of the Soviet Union and its social arrangements exercised a certain fascination on the subject peoples, who aspired to liberty and wished to enfranchise themselves away from external subordination. Violent disturbances were amply promised, and unless there was a minimum of pacification in the colonial areas very little metropolitan interest could be served by hanging on. But by granting independence two interests might still be served. First, the economic interest might still be served, as economic independence cannot be so quickly won as political independence. Indeed, the metropolitan economic interest could possibly be even better served through the granting of independence than in a situation of political subjection. At the same time, the granting of political independence could be used in the attempt to argue that the West and its faith was superior to the East and its faith. It could be used in an attempt to show territories which might yield to Russian persuasion, that capitalism could be generous. Of course, the subject peoples though concerned with political independence for itself, have also seen it as a pre-condition of economic and other successes. The generosity of the West should therefore also make itself felt in economic and other fields.

To take another example, perhaps peculiar to France, the Empire could be given away so that the greatness of a country and its influence might be seen by all. France might have wanted, for example, to show in the United Nations that its membership of the Security Council was validated by some influence in the General Assembly. And there is little doubt that this was so when the African empire, segmented by the *loi-cadre*, was first given its independence. The shock of Guinea consisted not in having sought immediate independence, which could be obtained at any time after the referendum, but by the defiance and repudiation of a glory-minded France.

Feelings of kinship have also been involved. And where there has been an appreciable settler-factor, metropolitan powers have dragged their feet noticeably.

It was believed before the first world war that people everywhere would come to adopt liberal democracy, because, it was thought, this was a natural form of government, and, since it was natural, it was inevitable. The question, as many thought, was one of time. There was a law of political evolution, inexorably moving all peoples towards liberal democracy, even if, like God, it must remain content with working in mysterious ways, its wonders to perform. There was an American capitalist earlier on in this century, perhaps a few, who let us know that the good God in His infinite mercy and inscrutable wisdom had entrusted the welfare of the many to his and a few other deserving capitalist hands. In the same way, if peoples elsewhere were rather laggardly about coming to the liberal democratic viewpoint, it became the duty of metropolitan powers to lead them, albeit slowly, but still surely, to this happy state of affairs. One held power in trust for subject peoples until they could be brought up to a condition in which they would freely embrace something like the Statute of Westminster as something which was theirs.

In more recent times, the story lost some of its well-to-do optimism. *Times* leaders in the inimitable style of that great paper lamented the retreat of democracy in the countries of Asia and Africa. They even speculated about chosen races. In their opinion, it appeared that the races of Asia and Africa had perhaps not been called to the democratic way of life. Liberal democracy, they concluded, was designed for Western Europe and the countries of the North American continent by name. *The Times* then did not believe that the countries of Africa and Asia could possibly base their claim to political independence on any interest or ability in propagating democracy. Democracy must then, perhaps, be practised for them to the little extent allowed by their perverse institutions, rampant illiteracy, and utter inability to think concretely, coherently, logically, and without sentiment. These would have been hard conclusions indeed.

One could not, of course, quite forget the setbacks that liberal democracy had suffered in Europe, where the evolution towards it might have been thought to be complete. There was that little matter of the Russian Revolution when, one supposes, a legitimate government of a country was overthrown by means not provided for in the liberal democratic view. Only wicked men sought to overthrow governments by means other than the ballot-box. And where the ballot-box did not exist, perhaps this was simply a misfortune. Anyway, no one really thought that Russia was really European. The Tsars indeed spoke French, and French, of course, is the language of Europe. But as to the others, some of them languished under a deep suspicion of being Asiatic.

When Mussolini, three years after the war, marched on Rome, only finicky minds were really distressed by the motion of evolution following devious paths.

And the French more recently have not altogether avoided methods of political action which degraded parliamentary rule, and showed no respect for the sincerity of the vote.

Confining oneself to the question of liberal democracy, one could ask two distinct questions. There is first the question of what its motivation is. There is then the question as to what means could be adopted to secure it.

Historically, its main motivation was the belief that popular government must coincide with good government. At least, since popular government would be an expression of the popular will, any criticism of it would be self-criticism. Conformably to this, one hears it said that a people get the government they deserve. Self-criticism, however, implies a desire to do better, and so craves the opportunity of so doing. Hence, the freely elected government must go to the electorate periodically to give everyone the opportunity of mending their ways if necessary. The only means of agitation allowed by liberal democracy are those which can plainly be described as peaceful—like writing letters to one's local representative in the government, or to newspapers, or marching in protest. Indefinite fasting would be a borderline case with the threat of moral blackmail. Gun-toting, arson, sabotage, are clearly out.

One wonders what form of agitation is open to a subject people without any governmental representation, as in Portuguese and Spanish territories, Algeria and South Africa, or where the representation is inadequate, as in the Central African Federation and Kenya.

In arguing against the granting of independence to subject peoples now, it has been said that freedom and liberal democracy, as ideals, first emerged in the West. It appears that what has been intended by this is that there are specific institutions and processes which make freedom secure and democracy possible in vast societies of many millions, and that it is among peoples of European stock that these have been initiated. If one places the emphasis on the size of the population then this remark hardly gives any weight to the claim about the origins of freedom and democracy. If one places the emphasis on the specific institutions and processes which are alone thought to make freedom secure and democracy possible, then one can also point at the palpable falsity of the claim. No institution or set of institutions can be identified with democratic ends, and there are none which, without reference to local conditions, can be said to be unique in securing democratic ends. The idea that there are institutions uniquely connected with democratic ends has, as regards Africa, been linked with two assertions. First, it is said that nationalism, in so far as it is a search for freedom and democracy, is of European introduction into Africa; there is, secondly, the assertion that Europe has nothing to learn from Africa, and so, as is sometimes said, the demand for self-government is the demand for the right to imitate the West. Hence, when arguments for and against the granting of self-government and independence are considered, one is really assessing how far the right to imitate the West can be conceded to colonies.

The ability of a people to govern themselves has been variously identified with four things. It has been said to be the ability to afford to modern trade and industry the security they need. Lurking behind this is the economic doctrine of man. Modern trade and industry are presumably here conceived to be modern Western trade and industry. It must be anomalous if the ability of a people to govern themselves has to be measured in terms of the needs of others. The ability to offer to any trade or industry the security it needs, is not greater than the ability to maintain the forces of law and order, and is in fact ancillary to it. Paradoxically, the criterion seems to identify, not the ability to govern oneself, but the spirit of colonialism. And it seems also to reveal the crystallisation of the metropolitan interest in economic matters, which permits the granting of political independence if economic interests in the subject territories are not thereby damaged.

The second account, as misguided as the first, traces the capacity of subjects for self-government to the ability to afford security of person and good government by the standards of Western Europe. Western Europe would here do with a little definition, as the chances of security of person and good government are not equally distributed. Both the rights of Western European citizens and the governmental practices vary according to where one is in Western Europe or America. And there are subject areas in Africa where citizens enjoy deeper rights than their opposite numbers do in Portugal or Spain or parts of the Deep South of the USA.

Third, it is said that the capacity for self-government is the ability to produce native rulers strong enough to respect international law. One wonders whether weakness is not a motive for respecting international law. There is some international law which every country, including, one supposes, even South Africa, respects. Fourth, and most tendentious, it is said that this capacity is nothing but the ability to work the institutions which make democracy and freedom effective.

Of institutions, it is safe to say that they have a point and reasons which make them effective. The designing of political institutions has always called for some exercise in conceptual thinking. Under the guidance of political theory and philosophy, political institutions are fashioned, and they are fashioned out of local resources and conditions. As local conditions and resources change, political theory recommends parallel changes in institutions in such a way that the proximity of abiding theoretical ideals is not reduced, but is maintained, or increased. In the case of subject countries, too, the same necessities which base political institutions on local resources operate, and their institutions must take account of local conditions in order to be effective and retain their integrity. The historical circumstances of Africa are not the same as those of Europe. The implementation of ideals through institutions can therefore be expected to call for skills different in some ways from those which Europeans and Americans enjoy today in their own *milieux*. This realisation is one that Africa and Asia can bring home to Europe, that different institutions can be devised to accommodate the same ideals in different circumstances. Indeed, the institutions of the West are themselves different among themselves, no doubt due to the different prevailing conditions.

When one enquires what the institutions and processes are which, uniquely, make freedom secure and democracy possible, one finds that they usually include an impartial judiciary, an efficient civil service, constitutional government, well-organised parties, pressure-groups, and a free press. Though these institutions do not define democracy, it could be hard to avoid some of them. Whether a society is atomistic or communalistic, based on a system of individual rights or a system of duties, democracy will be difficult for it without a judiciary which is reasonably impartial. Complete impartiality is too much to expect this side of the stateless society. Democracy is rational, for it removes the arbitrary and the gratuitous. And the impartial is rational. Impartiality is, besides, fundamentally egalitarian. An efficient civil service is also an instrument for reducing the role of the arbitrary and the gratuitous. But when a civil service becomes a bureaucracy, its fear of being arbitrary has become neurotic, and it is itself autocratic. Constitutional government is a like instrument. Well-organised parties, in the plural, are not essential to democracy. If a plurality of parties is essential, then, at least, a strong opposition party too is essential.

Where there are strong conflicting interests which also range widely over the population, the organisation of parties is a sensible means of diminishing the arbitrary and the gratuitous. But there is a point in this only when there is at least one opposition party or a set of opposition parties in unity which could offer a real threat to the ruling party before the electorate. The strong and well-organised interests of an extreme minority do not justify the creation of a party which seeks to rule a whole nation. It is clearly not inconceivable that a nation with a small population should almost wholly be in agreement on large national issues. It is as arbitrary and unreasonable to force people to form several parties as it is to force them to form just one. An organised opposition is not a presupposition of people having interests, and alternative parties are strongest when they begin naturally. The Governor of Tanganyika a few years ago summoned Julius Nyerere and said to him: 'Look here, Nyerere. You say you want independence. But where is your Opposition? You can't have independence without an Opposition.' To this Nyerere fittingly replied: 'But your Excellency, I cannot organise an Opposition to myself.'

It is clear that with the bare emergence of a plurality of parties, independence is not going to be handed over. It could therefore be much better for all involved to join their efforts together in a movement for independence. When a majority party presses for independence there is nothing left for a minority party to do, but to retard or otherwise compromise the national effort. It is possible, of course, that the majority party should be less militant than the minority party; but this depends on the co-operation of the metropolitan power. Voting according to party lines, where there are no fundamental philosophical, religious, or ideological rifts, has, before independence has been attained, the effect of dividing Africa in flippant and unserious ways, and has attenuated the force of the public conscience over electoral issues. Where political differences are not programmatic, but centre on priorities, or even personalities; where, as in an under-developed country with not a very high literacy percentage, there is no surfeit of men of ability, and no political party has the monopoly of them such as

145

they are, to treat schismatic forces like a fetish becomes, at least, ill-considered.

Sometimes, a party is the political expression of a class or a bracket of classes, and here, when the country is not faced with national crises, a class party in power quietly settles down to fortifying its interest. Even in moments of national crises, it usually finds time to do something for its sectional interest. In traditional Africa, the differentiation of classes did not imply a diversification of political interest, or interest fortifiable by political action. Much less did it imply an opposition between such interests. Objectives, when political, were communal in interest, and methods were, if not always directly communal, at least communally sanctioned. It is possibly for this reason that there have been African patriots who have deprecated the growth of political parties as distinct from movements. Something of the same feeling must be detected in the earnest assiduity with which successful political parties have been extending themselves in the proportions of movements.

The present problems of Africa offer even less motive for awkward schismatic urges. They concern unity and progress, and the unity of Africa is more important for this, continental-wise and regionally, than the sovereignty of any region. It cannot be that while the rest of the world feel their interest threatened, and behave as if they had swallowed nettles, a godfatherly destiny should arrange that Africa alone should be untroubled by problems. Others have sought solutions, or minimally, amelioration of their problems through larger groupings for purposes varying between the military, the economic, and the political. Will the uniqueness of Africa discover a new method? Africa can count its blessings. The genius required for solving her problems in disunity is not one of them.

Where there is a single party, it does not follow that there is internal homogeneity of interest and articulation. And the reconciliation which articulate sectional interests within a party could produce is more significant for the democracy and peace of a nation than any impression which a weak opposition can make. The presence of a weak but vociferous opposition before independence is attained could lead to intolerance and harshness on all sides. An opposition, to be sensible, in this context, must be strong and have a chance of winning.

The tendency in Africa today is undoubtedly towards one-party states. In some areas, opposition parties have been banned. Elsewhere, majority parties are so overwhelmingly large that opposition parties might just as well not exist. The regional division of French Africa, which the *loi-cadre* achieved, in fact attained stability only through conglomeration of limbs into unified parties. Guinea is perhaps the most striking of the complete examples. In Mali, too, parties were freely united and without violence. The coalitions, e.g. in Haute-Volta under the gifted Ovezzin Coulibaly, in Dahomey, and in Tchad under the also gifted Boganda, were weaker than the frankly one-party states. In Ivory Coast and Senegal, the majorities were almost complete. In Ghana and Sierra Leone, the majorities are effectively complete. This is true also of Tanganyika which gains independence in December. In Nigeria, the regional majorities are overwhelming and almost complete in the northern region, the federal structure being, perhaps, the single crucial factor in preserving the balance of forces.

Pressure-groups operating not openly, but behind the scenes, are undemocratic. A pressure-group is, if anything, a minority that seeks to exert the force of a majority. Its interests are special, and though in a hierarchy of national interests those of a particular pressure-group may come first, they should operate, being seen to be such. They should not become mystical. When they do, they conflict with the impartiality of the democratic process.

The last item mentioned in connection with the essential institutions and processes of democracy was a free press. In its application to questions of independence, it is said that subject countries in Africa are largely illiterate. At best, the arguments involved here can be put as follows: a free and well-informed press is useless to an illiterate people; consequently, since a free and well-informed press is essential to democracy, an illiterate people cannot make democracy work. Though access to information and freedom of discussion are important to democracy, they can be guaranteed in other ways than through a free and well-informed press. Sound radio, television, the cinema, even gong-beating by street-criers in villages, or gossip —any of these is better than a free press in an illiterate society. An illiterate society has its own methods of disseminating news and information. A free and well-informed press is a device peculiarly suited to a literate people. If one looks closely at the press of the world, one soon realises that very little, compared to what is possible, really goes on in the press by way of spreading true and accurate information, by way of leading public opinion to virtue, by way of fortifying democracy. In many ways, in Great Britain, it is the *Daily Mirror* and not *The Times* or the *Telegraph*, and hardly the ambiguous *Guardian*, which comes anywhere near achieving this. The *Daily Mirror* is not gentlemanly about thinking right about principles on occasion. It speaks with a directness towards the ideals of democratic intentions, unwarped by pressure groups, which is often moving. In France, *Le Monde* comes nearest to this. Where the percentage of literacy is very small, a free press also presented a certain risk, the risk of its being unduly concerned with the interests of the literate group, which naturally tends to coalesce into a class in a Marxian sense. A free press among a minority does not secure Aristotle's idea, that notion according to which the whole truth is never within the purview of one man, but is made up of contributions by different men who grasp different parts and aspects of it.

When one speaks of an illiterate people, it is well to be somewhat clear about terms. In the minds of many, illiteracy among a subject people appears to be equated with illiteracy in some metropolitan vernacular. There are, of course, an indefinite number of persons in some subject and formerly subject countries who are by no means illiterate in their own languages, however innocent they may stand of French, or Spanish, or Portuguese, or English.

Subject peoples have been talked about as though they were *tabulae rasae*, on which metropolitan countries make their impression. It is sometimes said that it would be better for the process of westernisation or easternisation to go very far in order that subject peoples should be able to find their bearings before they are left to their own devices as independent peoples. Westernisation in some areas may well relate more to techniques and skills than to the realm of values, which is after all that realm by reference to which one assesses the value of skills. It is possible indeed to conceive an independent country which has its own view of things, and borrowing certain skills from another society, in such a way that these already stand reconciled to the larger framework, and so in such a way that there is no question of now finding one's bearings. It might, of course, be said that the process of westernisation is not a process of choice. In some measure, this is true. But it is not implied that the degree of westernisation, its possible effects, and its standing with what is indigenous, cannot be discerned, or that westernisation cannot be controlled. Westernisation can in fact be deliberate. It is subject to decision. What goes for westernisation goes for easternisation.

In areas where there are European settlers, the British and the French have been somewhat coy about the prospects of independence. The Spanish and the Portuguese appear not to have thought of the substantive question itself. In discussing the independence of African areas where there are European settlers, one must bear it in mind that democracy was not invented for the comfort of the minority. To hedge it round with devices designed purely to please minorities, is to go beyond rejecting democracy's egalitarian basis, and helping the few to triumph over the many. The attribution of special rights to minorities, outside the general framework of common rights, which therefore exceeds the legitimate interests of minorities, is contrary to democracy. One distinguishing mark of democracy is that such adventitious characteristics as the colour of the skin, or the home of ancestors a century ago, carry no distinction or privilege with them.

The system of differential franchise, devised by a political genius, is also quite destructive of democracy, and of the human spirit. The limitation of the franchise to people of at least twenty-one is a traditional limitation which accords well with the legal responsibilities of majors. But when franchise is based, say, on middle age, this becomes arbitrary. It is at least very hard to conceive any relevant sudden access of responsibility and wisdom which befalls one in middle age, and the absence of which at twenty-one unfits one for the vote. A universal adult suffrage has a built-in validity in the term 'adult'; but whoever heard of such a grotesque thing as a universal middle age suffrage? Everyone knows that these inventions are related to the preservation of the privilege of settlers. Inevitably, the African countries of Kenya, Nyasaland, Northern Rhodesia, Southern Rhodesia, Angola, Mozambique, Spanish Africa, Algeria, and South Africa will all become independent. The settlers will stay. There is not the slightest likelihood of a mass exodus of Europeans and Asians from Africa. They are too deeply involved to cut the Gordian knot in this way. This fact, however, makes it seem paradoxical that the present favoured minority positions should be propped up by arbitrary and differential means; for it must be supposed that even minorities seek to live in Africa in security and peace. Special safeguards only breed resentment. Skills will continue to be regarded very highly in Africa, and the possession of skills is everywhere a natural insurance for their owners. Minorities without skills are safeguarded in the fact that they can have nothing to lose.

It is also sometimes said that where settlers are grossly outnumbered by indigenous Africans, extending the franchise simply to the latter would be to rob settlers of Africa. It is commonly said that not only has the settler lived in Africa for several generations, he has also raised Africa to what it is today from bare earth and rock. If settlers have lived in Africa for several generations, Africans have lived there for countless centuries. And when one says that the settler has built Africa, does one take facts of labour into account? Touching this, one might recollect that in South Africa labour strikes are illegal on the part of Africans. It is, of course, not European sweat and toil that has built Africa, but African. Europeans have admittedly contributed great skills. But literally, it is Africans who have built Africa. And it is of course Africans who will continue to build it.

It is a tenet of African nationalism that political independence is a condition of economic, social, cultural, and so spiritual strength. This belief is, of course, contradicted by supporters of the Central African Federation. To be sure, the idea of a federation does not necessarily imply any evils. There are citable federations which have diffused greatness, prosperity and stability around their members. Admitting this, one can still realise that between the conception and the act falls the shadow. The main arguments advanced in favour of the Central African Federation are, first, that it will bring prosperity to the Africans, and second, that it will both prevent Southern Rhodesia from moving into the Union of South Africa, and prevent the general area from succumbing to communism. Southern Rhodesia was not doing very well economically when the Federation came into being. It needed more docile and cheaper labour. The swelling of the market with the unemployed of Nyasaland, mainly, was therefore a gratifying chance for Southern Rhodesia, and for the copperbelt of Northern Rhodesia too. The imposition of Federation without the approval and against the wishes of the Africans, who outnumbered the Europeans by 184 to 1, has not, as everyone can see, exactly ushered the seven million Africans into the affluent society. The economic benefits which have accrued have accrued in the main to the settler population. On this score, the Federation has failed grotesquely. One recalls that the running of Nyasaland and Northern Rhodesia as separate countries before the Federation had not actually depleted the British Treasury. It was certainly not possible to argue that any deficits in their budgets would be removed by Federation.

Southern Rhodesia has never been very far from the Union of South Africa, and apartheid was sometimes carried to more absurd lengths in the former, as when an only African female undergraduate was obliged to have a whole hall of residence to herself. The African Affairs Board, which Oliver Lyttleton described as an impregnable bastion, has been stultified; and Welensky, with disarming openness and frankness, appears to have achieved its abolition. The Federation cannot be supported by fair argument, by sentiment, or by loyalty. Indeed, it has fallen so short of its promises that it arouses wonder whether it ever intended to fulfil them. The greatest danger to the

Africans is that independence should be given to the countries of the Federation before Africans have acceded to the positions of power.

Essentially, colonialism is aggression.

In the pursuit of independence, one should not be ashamed of appearing extremist. Ghandi, for example, was an extremist in his uncompromising and triumphant attitude, as uncompromising as it was non-violent. Wherever possible, the pursuit of independence should, as a counsel of prudence, proceed with non-violent means. But these non-violent means can be carried to extremes, and often require so to be carried to become effective. The European idea of man today is that he is an economic animal, and it is this account of man that African nationalists must largely refer to in their efforts for independence. Non-violent means which threaten the economic position of settlers will be appreciated with greater promptitude than dialectics. In the colonial countries of Algeria, South Africa, Angola, Mozambique and Spanish Africa, it will require ultimate orders of ingenuity to seek independence through non-violent means, foresighted governments having taken the precaution of outlawing these in advance. In Algeria, strikes are not illegal. Fortunately, peaceful and democratic agitation is still possible elsewhere even if its progress is slow and painful.

African nationalism is not racialist, though race questions force themselves into it. African nationalism in its external aspect is directed mainly at the fortification of independence or the regaining of it. Essentially, the system whereby the political volition of one people is made to lie entirely in that of another, regards or treats the former people as being unable or without the right to decide the government under which they shall live. An attempt to apply the economic analysis of man to Africa has failed. In Africa, man has not traditionally been analysed as an economic animal. When it was said that a hungry people did not bother its head about democracy, this apophthegm did not soothe independence demands, and only betrayed frightful cynicism. It is not true that every man has his price. The subjection of one people by another is hardly brought about from philanthropic motives, and the story is told of the lady who went to Colonial India and admitted that, frankly, life without a subject race would be intolerable.

In the eighteenth and nineteenth centuries, a number of theorists thought they could detect the emergence of the truly rational man, a universal man in knowledge and sentiment, freed from his regional and narrow loyalties. His actions were to be based on the idea of the universal brotherhood of man, without differentiation. The hope of the emergence of this kind of man in political life appears to have been set back by the latter half of the nineteenth century and our own century. Those who disliked this international man thought him to be ruthless, too cerebral, too intellectualist, cut off from the warm fullness of life. Those who liked him thought that the resurgence of nationalistic feeling was an atavism or even barbarism.

The idea of the universal brotherhood of man has not been completely lost. It survives in the United Nations Organisation, the World Bank, and other international agencies.

Nationalism, even when it reverts to roots, is, of course, not an atavism or barbarism. It can be reconciled with internationalism. Indeed, internationalism presupposes nationalism, and the latter ensures that development and progress in the world shall be on a broad front.

Naturally, it is when schismatic forces might be rather strong that nationalism mentions common roots. The interest in the roots is certainly historical, but it is also practical. It creates a basis for commonness of purpose. The existence of diverse languages in active use among regions of the same country could lead to schisms unless an ulterior identity is revealed. The ulterior identity admittedly owes something to the fact that regions were colonially administered as one country. But it can be more significantly based on a unity of culture. A common purpose is more important to nationalism than a common origin.

African nationalism is militant without being aggressive or chauvinistic. The transportation from tribalism through regionalism to pan-Africanism is some confirmation of this. If it were aggressive or chauvinistic, African nationalism would get stuck at the regional level. Nationalism need not produce a closed society. Naturally, nationalism will include something mythical. There is always an element of myth in a culture, and nationalism, when it deals with origins, is in its greatest danger of involving myth. Vinobha Bhavan, to break some of the exclusiveness and puritanism that uncontrolled nationalism might lead to, has changed his mode of greeting from 'Hail, India!' to 'Hail, universe!'!

The Soviets have naturally not been unconcerned with events in Africa. Indeed, to a certain extent, they had anticipated some of the events. Their two theories of evolution were applied directly to Africa. One theory of evolution concerns societies, the other concerns individuals. The former lays down for societies a pattern of development which moves classically from the primitive commune to the slave-owning society, through feudalism, through the capitalist system to socialism, the penultimate to paradisiac communism. Soviet historians have been a little inconclusive about the rigidity of these stages. Some indeed vaguely hint that in certain circumstances, a telescoping of stages may take place. In illustration, it is maintained that Eastern Slavs passed directly from the primitive commune to the feudal system. And within the Soviet Union itself, it is said that some of its underdeveloped territories were hurricaned by revolutionary dynamics from a feudal to a socialist structure. A number of purists, however, refuse to make any concessions, and, as against Grekov, Zhukov is adamant on the inevitability of the Marxist-Leninist schedule.

Of man, the Soviet theory of evolution holds that he begins as a creature without power over natural phenomena, in dread of which he spends his life. To contain this dread, and, if possible, overcome it, man develops a belief in magic and in magicians. Religion is dismissed as the sophistication of magic, and itself suffers a metamorphosis from animism to monotheism. Idealist conceptions of society and nature and the belief in revealed religion are soon abandoned, and all is now set for a transition to rationality. Rationality, it is supposed, is entirely materialistic, and is incompatible with religious belief.

Soviet opinions on Africa have been guided by two attitudes

to the continent, the attitude to Africa as a number of substantive societies revealing different aspects of the Marxian dialectic, and the attitude to Africa as an effect of Europe. The two theories of evolution were applied to Africa within the first attitude, and for the second attitude guidance was obtained from Lenin's *Imperialism*. Wearing the evolutionist spectacles, the Soviets saw Africa as being in the nineteenth century a number of societies in which the tribe was already beginning to wither away. Though rich men and poor men had emerged, they were not thought to form rival classes, communal affairs having been presided over by clan groups. According to the Soviets, there were no state organisations. Great admiration has been shown by them for Chaka's and Dingaan's heroism, Chaka in forging out a unified military empire and Dingaan in striving after centralisation. In these changes, the Soviets claimed to see a fulfilment of the Marxist-Leninist evolutionary schedule. All everybody needed to do would have been to sit back and wait for the dialectical process to spend itself, had not imperialism, alas, swooped in like a vulture. And so, the Soviets say, the natural process, in spite of its ineluctability, was effectively interfered with by European colonisation and imperialist land policies, through which ethnic groups were territorially sub-divided and split apart. The gloom of the Soviets is a little perplexing at this point, for they appear to think that colonial rule has in fact inserted a transition almost from the primitive commune ignoring wide dialectical chasms and gorges direct to capitalistic forms. May not the pace of evolution be forced every now and then?

In the attempt to salvage the schematic schedule which an unhurrying and inflexible historic process has chosen for itself, the Soviets treated African traditional land tenure systems as being, in the main, feudal, on the score, apparently, that instead of making exclusive use of terms like those of purchase and sale, work and wages, they introduce concepts of usage, right and obligation. The preservation of the analysis of chiefship was another motive in calling the African traditional systems feudal. The motive force of the evolutionary process was, of course, moral, for it aimed at the obliteration of injustice from stage to stage. The injustice was unfortunately persistently conceived in economic terms. And the analysis of chiefship was itself economic. In calling the traditional system feudal, with the economic disproportion that this entailed, it was possible for the Soviets to accept their economic, but no charismatic, account of chiefship. The chief immediately appeared as a source of continuing economic un-redress.

At this point the Soviets run against a fact which is upsetting for them. This is the strength of traditional forces in Africa. They had had to acknowledge that the chief was the instrument of the greater consolidation which feudalism represented over the primitive commune. This advance in organisation required, in Soviet theory, to be matched by a parallel advance towards realism, towards rationality. And rationality the Soviets dumped in the tub of economics. The approximation towards rationality which feudalism represented over the primitive commune was reflected in the economic, rather than charismatic, analysis of the feudalistic chief.

The Soviets saw the continuing significance of the chief as part of the surviving traditional forces. They, however, suspected that chiefship had been deliberately propped up for imperialist purposes, more so in British Africa than in French, Portuguese, Spanish or Belgian. All these nations, except the British, had been content to rule Africa directly. The British, with a sensitive, if prominent, nose for subtle changes, devised indirect rule through local chiefs, and so, instead of wasting energy fighting deep-rooted traditional forces, used them. They had their sensible social anthropologists, including Rattray, to thank for this. Lugard made use of a social-anthropological discovery. The under-prop which the Colonial Administration in British Africa provided for chiefship has not been rated too highly by the Soviets. They believe that the complex of religious attitudes on which traditional Africa is founded ranks higher in explaining the social dynamic of chiefs. They have singled out the emirates of Northern Nigeria and Houphuet-Boigny's government of the Ivory Coast for special groans.

The traditional forces have not alone irked the Soviets. The intelligentsia have sometimes caused worry, and still do in

China's mind. It is true that the internal contradictions of capitalism and imperialism, expressed in relation to colonies in conflicts among the imperial powers, had been expected to shatter imperialism, but the Soviets in this instance thought that the evolutionary process should be assisted by revolutions. Of the conflicts among capitalist powers, the Soviets might have pointed with some glee, in spite of the Berlin Conference and the partition of Africa, at the efforts of the United States of America to thwart French designs on the independence of Liberia towards the end of the last century.

It was not thought that national liberation could be achieved through legal means. Of course, the truth of this would have to depend on the actual content of law in any given area. There are methods of agitation which are legitimate, but not necessarily legal. Non-co-operation is legitimate, and while it has been legal in British Africa, in Portuguese, Spanish, and Belgian Africa it has been illegal. In South Africa the weight of the Suppression of Communism Act is brought to bear on it. The Soviets recommended a positive revolution in a military sense. They thought this to be essential. This recommendation is no longer stressed by them, and it has been frankly negated by Khrushchev.

The treachery and instability of bourgeois revolutions, by which the Soviets appear to mean revolution by round-table conference, are still believed in in the communist world. That a bourgeois leadership of a national revolution is capable of treachery to the revolution and instability is, of course, unquestionable. But to make this possibility a ground of hostility to it is neurotic. The insistence that only working classes are in any given society dedicated to national liberation and capable of carrying it through is connected with the Soviet misapprehension of the possibilities of revolutions. In Africa, no political revolution can be successful without the support of workers. But workers are not the whole of the revolution. Ideas about the possibilities of revolutions were lodged in Lenin's nationalities policy. Revolution in that policy was the world proletarian revolution, and provision was made for the suppression of national aspirations when they came in conflict, as in Hungary, with the needs of the world proletarian revolution. According to the policy, nationalism had to content itself with the substitution of ethnic and linguistic processes for political ones. Its issue was Stalin's 1923 slogan, 'Socialist in content, national in form.'

Soviet attitudes towards African nationalist movements and the pan-African movement have accordingly been unstable. The move to break the finger of imperialism was welcomed in the belief that it would weaken capitalism, or at least be an ideal springboard for engineering the discomfiture of capitalism. The protagonists of the nationalist movements appeared at times to be cast in unbelievable roles. Consolation was found by the Soviets in the fact that the roles were interesting. The diversion of energies towards pan-Africanism has, however, not always pleased the Soviets any more than it has pleased the West. To the former, the trend represented a threat to leap out of the world proletarian revolution groove, instead of carrying on with the main task of putting imperialism and capitalism out of face everywhere. In this way the Soviets have tended to see pan-Africanism romantically as being concerned more with the liquidation of the West than with African reconstruction. To the West, pan-Africanism is odious because a united Africa could pose a direct economic threat to her, while a discreet Africa would have to weaken itself through competition for favours.

In Lenin's nationalities policy, an attempt was in fact made to extend to the world what only applied to nations. There are multi-national empires, multi-national commonwealths, multi-national alliances, multi-national ideologies; but there is no such thing as a multi-national state. There are only national states. The attempt to treat sub-groups within a state as a national group is treacherous to the basis of the state. This is what France has tried to secure in Algeria, and what unsteadies Britain's hand in Kenya, Northern Rhodesia and Southern Rhodesia, in the handling of settler problems.

Politically, most of Africa is independent now; on purely political questions it has a certain sense of initiative. But when political matters have a critical effect on economic prospects, policy has not fully reflected independence. A great deal of importance comes to be associated with the friendly smiles one can raise outside Africa. It used to be commonly said in Africa that the eyes of the whole world were upon us. The effect of this on action was that it depleted it of sincerity and balance. The eyes of the whole world are not on Africa. If the eyes of Africa could be turned inwards, however, and bootless comparisons with other continents indulged in less, the African miracle might take place. The independence of Africa will not amount to much unless Africa can be egocentric in action and self-image.

CHAPTER 4

AFRICA REDIVIVA

*Economic Problems: Economic resources—Virtue of African unity—
Political problems—The Revolutionary Party: Identity quests—
Problems of Government—Role of Intellectuals: Neutralism: The
British Commonwealth—Revolution and ethics: Aims of education—
African renaissance—Pan Africanism.*

AFRICA, OF COURSE, HAS a great deal for which to be thankful. It
must be grateful that the slave trade, having been established,
was in the end abolished; it must be grateful for schools, for
education, for scientific medicine and scientific agriculture and
the control of pests; it must be grateful to missionaries for their
work of evangelisation, reformation, education, and medicine;
to the explorers for making possible the opening up of the
continent and its more effective integration through vastly
improved communications; to several government officials for
their selfless administrative work.

This expression of gratitude must not suggest that Europe
was in Africa for Africa's health. It must not, in particular,
obscure the fact that some of the present problems of Africa
are needless consequences of the contact with Europe. Many
of the problems arise largely from the absence of planning
and of any seriousness about the values and native institutions
of Africa. The attitude to Africa was, from Africa's viewpoint,
casual, amateurish, unprincipled. Europe also brought racialism
into Africa.

In response to the economic theory of man, British and
French Colonialism has been greatly amended. In Algeria and
Kenya, the delay in the granting of independence is almost
altogether founded on economic fears, fears of dispossession of

the white minorities by enfranchising African majorities. A redistribution of natural resources would probably be necessary in these two countries, come independence; for that is the means to one particular social justice at present lacking in both areas. All that is left is that the politicians in these areas should buy their independence with guarantees of compensation in cases of readjustment involving the dispossession of white minorities.

The future of Africa rests on the present, and the present is an outcome of the past. By the present, one wishes to indicate the resultant of the operation of the forces of traditional Africa and the forces which the contact with Europe has unleashed upon the continent. One must be clear in some detail about the culture with which Europe has been in touch in order to be able to give the right formulation to problems. Right formulations will facilitate correct diagnosis. And a prescription which grows out of the diagnosis has the best chance of optimum success.

Intertwined with the resources of Africa are the problems of Africa. Some of the problems may, so to say, be called substantial, and some adjectival. The adjectival problems are those involved in the type and the pace of changes which Africa is suffering today. The problems of change in Africa have caught the attention of sociologists, anthropologists, educators, doctors, psychologists, psychiatrists, nurses, churches, governments, administrators. The symptomatology of the strenuous reactions involved in the changes is naturally produced by the local cultures of Africa, and unless one can analyse these correctly, action is not soundly based. Unless traditional cultures, which continue to be effective, can be accommodated as steadying influences, progress, instead of being continuous and rational, will become gibbous.

The problems which are involved in these changes may be categorised as economic, political, social, and educational. The progress of Africa will depend on Africa's ability both to appreciate problems and to solve them.

In addition to introducing new possibilities in economics, politics, social organisation and education into Africa, Europe has had a distintegrative effect. Disintegration has come with the Christian religion, European economics, communication systems, European law and government. The Christian religion, with its emphasis on the accountability of the individual conscience to God, has had a disruptive effect. The economic organisation, with its tying of reward to individual effort; road, rail, water and air communications, increasing the range and speed of contact, and hence the rate of culture contact and change; the administration of a number of tribes together as a territorial unit, with the opportunities of migrations so created —all these have had a disruptive effect on the organisation of the family and the clan. The introduction of wage-earning activities alone has interfered with the traditional connections between family life, division of labour and property; family bonds have been weakened through migrations in pursuit of wages, and there has also in consequence been an increase in polygamy, as wives in general are not taken around in the labour migrations.

The variegations in the problems in Africa even when they have been categorised are due to an appreciable extent to the differences in policies of Britain, which was responsible for four million square miles, France—also responsible for four million square miles, Belgium with one million square miles, Portugal with 750,000 square miles, and Spain with 170,000 square miles. The British policy was from the time of Macaulay one of an approach to eventual independence, albeit a gradual approach. The idea was that the British civilisation should be cultivated by graft on to the African cultures, traditions, languages, and, where possible, ideals. France had a diametrically opposed policy. It believed in a centralised type of colonial government. It discouraged chiefship, as having no role to play in the assimilation of France's colonies to France. France saw her subjects as falling into an élite group and an indigenous group. The élite received a thoroughly French education, learnt French usages, and became Frenchmen. The indigenes received an impoverished education at what were referred to as schools of initiation. The French therefore believed in standardisation and the British did not. Belgium followed a line that was similar to France's line in its distinction between an élite and the indigenes. But it saw its African territories purely as a possession. There was neither the French hope to assimilate the colonies with the metropolitan country, nor the British intention of leaving them on their own feet at some distant date. The education which Belgium offered her territories rose little above the elementary school. The Portuguese and Spanish home régimes continue to see their African territories as one of their natural resources, and they are exploited with the impersonality, and, in this case, the brutality that one has towards natural resources. And the same was true of Germany when she was a colonial power in Africa.

These differences in attitude towards Africa survive today in the pattern and gravity of problems involved in change in the new Africa.

The reasons why Africa has suddenly become independent and so finds herself loaded with problems for which she has not even adumbrated solutions are evidently not rooted in the colonial policies of the metropolitan powers, for even with the eight points of the Atlantic Charter which Britain admitted to apply to Africa, speculation about the coming of political independence was in terms of sixty to one hundred years. Likewise in an article in *Time and Tide* for February 10th, 1940, on 'The Future of the Colonies', there appeared a prophetic deposition, somewhat anticipating the Atlantic Charter, in which the author, Dr W. B. Mumford, broached a sixty-year plan. And even the American Committee on Africa, the War and Peace Aims, sitting in 1942, hardly expected that the generation of Kwame Nkrumah, Ako Adjei, Ross Lohr, Ibanga Udo Akpabio—men from Ghana, Sierra Leone, and Nigeria whom it had asked to submit memoranda—would claim and obtain independence for Africa.

In a series of two articles called 'America and the Empire' published in *The Times* in 1942, Margery Perham considers the dangers of misunderstanding of the British and the need for definitions. Pursuing the latter, she writes:

'Is it too much to hope that a voice might be heard from this country with the ring of leadership proclaiming a clear plan of advance that would catch the imagination of the common man in Britain and in the Colonies and give them the sense of working together to achieve it? There are difficulties and risks in proclaiming plans. But today there are difficulties and risks in not proclaiming them. This language would be understood in America and help to win that full co-operation without which it is so difficult to foresee the re-establishment of the lost territories or the future well-being of Empire or Commonwealth. These words will be called defeatism by some. It is rather realism to recognize the relative reduction in our world position, which is something quite different from an absolute decline. Our position will be stronger if we shift our stance from unsound planks to firm ones.'

It is probable that there were three conditions which have made the political agitation in Africa for national independence successful. The possession of colonies in Africa by a number of European powers, some of them as weak as Spain and Portugal, to the exclusion of a potentially powerful nation like Germany, was a constant irritant to war. Malinowski had pointed out that it was not accidental that the scramble for Africa followed the Industrial Revolution. The scramble for Africa ensured for Europe the control of the resources and cheap labour of Africa. In this, Europe was considerably assisted by Americans imbued with financial and commercial interests. But for American support, the Congo, for example, would not have passed into Leopold's pocket. Europe found in Africa a vast source of raw materials and a yielding market. Germany could not allow the loss of her share in these after the First World War, to persist unremedied. The dissolution of the empires appeared as an alternative to a new scramble for Africa. Besides, the empires were proving too vast for simultaneous defence.

The bearing of Russia as a new world power, and a vastly odious one to the West, has already been indicated. The influence of America on the empire-owning countries has in effect not been much different from that of the Russians. The success of the West in separating political independence from economic independence must naturally be accounted a catalyst.

Now that Africa has assured herself of her political independence with the accompanying problems categorised as economic, political, social, and educational, it rests with her to decide what to do about them and how to handle them.

Some of the economic problems have been quite incidental to the eruption of territories into statehood. Those economic problems attendant on urbanisation, for example, may be accounted such. In Africa, urbanisation has not been generally accompanied by industrialisation. Elsewhere, industrialisation has been a cause of urbanisation. The absence of this link in Africa raises questions about the economic capacity of cities to support continually growing populations. Many of the migrants to the cities have come to earn money and remit it to their villages. This has meant that only a fraction of their earnings, such as they are, is available for their own immediate use. Not infrequently, they consequently settle on the periphery of large towns in buildings largely improvised. The spread of education is another factor leading to urbanisation in Africa, and there is the differential standard of living between rural and urban areas, and the preference for the latter which education breeds in one. The under-population of Africa combined with the primitive methods of agriculture and fishing reduces the food surpluses which are available to the large towns and cities. Africa is consequently in the ridiculous position, for her, of having to import food.

It is true that during the period of the loss of independence, economic activity in Africa increased stupendously, but its pattern was grotesque. African craftsmen were squeezed out. Though populations became more settled and even increased, the crafts did not enjoy a reasonable expansion in markets. There were cloth-weavers, spinners, dyers, bleachers, designers, builders, gold- and silver-smiths, blacksmiths, stool-makers. potters, fishermen, farmers. The stool-makers have now been supplemented with joiners and carpenters who enjoy a reasonable home market. The gold- and silver-smiths too enjoy a similar market. The cloth-weavers, concentrating on the more luxurious types of cloth, are succeeding in pricing themselves out. Europeans brought new goods into Africa, and more finished goods of the type found in Africa. These were purveyed by European traders who were able to pass back to Europe all the capital which might have accrued from industry and commerce. Monopolies with their accompanying arbitrary price-fixings developed, and little of the profits were re-invested in Africa in industries connected with the goods involved. Restrictive practices grew immeasurably as manufacturers let African traders know that they already had agents in Africa.

As to the industrial development of Africa, that too was left to private companies who showed some coyness about ploughing in capital as the rate of interest was not high enough. Direct investment held more promise. Social utility was relatively unimportant, hence communications were not developed on a national scale. Railways, roads, waterways were inadequately developed, the latter hardly at all. Instead a great deal of money was thrown into the pits in mines, from which private companies, not unreasonably, expected the quickest and the highest gains. In agriculture, effort was directed towards export rather than food for home consumption. Coffee, tea, cocoa, cotton, became intensely cultivated, and Africans continued to be undernourished. Africa is surrounded on all sides by oceans, but it had to import tinned fish. Japanese and European fleets fished off the West African coast, took their catches home, and re-exported them in red tins to West Africa! No manufacturing skills were developed. Labour was largely absorbed in extractive activity, on farms and in mines.

The economic needs of Africa are great. Africa needs schools, universities and technical colleges, hospitals, roads, railways, water supplies, electricity, food, and sheer wealth. The measure to which Africans can help themselves is inconsiderable, because personal incomes are low and prices are high. The state, therefore, has to provide services in a proportion unusual in many countries. The wealth to pay for them must therefore be produced. Africa must therefore find means of producing the wealth she wants.

The problems are so severe that only a radical solution can meet them. A radical solution means industrialisation. Industrialisation will also rationalise Africa's primary production. There are two possibilities of industrialisation open, an agricultural one and a manufacturing one. For either of these, Africa must assess her resources. Africa, with only two hundred million inhabitants to some eighteen million square miles, is in area the equivalent of Europe, the United States, India and China together. It is obvious that land as such cannot be a problem in Africa. Africa has deep, fertile soil in vast quantities. Its not so good soil can be converted through chemical means. It has forest resources, animals and also minerals. It has un-limited unskilled labour. In skilled labour and capital, it is grossly defective. For an agricultural industry, relatively to a manufacturing industry, very little is needed by way of skill.

In the forests of Central Africa, there is enough timber for African use and export. There is an abundance of dye woods and cabinet woods. The valleys, plains, and plateaux of Africa could be put to the cultivation of vegetables, grains, and fruits. Tobacco, potatoes, oats, barley, coffee, sugar, coco-nuts, veget-able oil plants, maize, yams, tomatoes, onions, peanuts, peppers, cocoa, rubber, cotton, and a host of other crops could be cultivated in Africa profusely. The cultivated acreage of East Africa alone could be made equivalent to that of the United States, and put under crops of the temperate zone for export. Through varying the types of available fruits, surpluses could be amassed for export. The West African pineapple, for example, is the best in the world, but it has no keeping qualities. If a way could be found of preserving it, it would find a soft export market.

These agricultural objectives would, of course, present their own problems, both technical and cultural. The technical problems can all be solved. Considering that a large proportion of African workers have been absorbed in non-food-producing labour, one realises that, barring cocoa, almost all of the peasant produce of Africa is absorbed in feeding wage-earners. There are certain agricultural practices which have not helped. The practice of shifting cultivation and extending acreages has impoverished the fertility of Africa in some areas. As acreages are increased, the surplus land diminishes, and the length of time for which a plot of land can be allowed to lie fallow and recover from exploitation is gravely reduced. Added to this is the depredation of soil erosion. Unless methods of vigorous soil-conservation and amelioratives through chemical fertilisers are urgently used, the indigenous agriculture of Africa will collapse. Improved methods of sowing, nurturing, and harvesting are needed for optimum crops. And since fertilisers are costly, compost can be used in large quantities as a measure of economy. Research has been carried out into crop sequences and rotations likely to prosper most in particular types of soil. Crop rotation was indeed a method of farming used by Africans before the European penetration. Maize, cotton, groundnuts and beans could form a cycle, for example. Crop rotation is an effective means of maintaining cash crops at optimum levels of price because of the seasonal factor, and also a means of minimising the truce in shifting cultivation.

The drier parts of Africa like the north of Ghana and Nigeria, Upper Volta, *et cetera*, are more suitable for grazing than for cultivation. Intensive animal husbandry in these areas, and in parts of Kenya and Tanganyika, could produce cattle for milk and meat, more than enough for Africa's needs. It is true that there are pastoral groups in Africa among whom cattle are prized per head rather than for produce, and whose semi-religious attitude to cattle would rule out any question of marketing. But enough cattle could be bred elsewhere in Africa. It is true also that cattle-rearing in Africa is bedevilled by diseases like black water, red water, gall-sickness, anthrax, rinderpest, east coast fever. But these can all be overcome by immunisation, or vaccination, or dipping and segregation. In Kenya and Uganda, where control of cattle disease is considerably advanced, the cattle population has considerably increased. Grazing problems can be solved by breeding the highest quality cattle for milk and meat, controlling grazing to prevent total loss of such facilities through debilitating the fields, and by creating pasture land in bare areas. Irrigation systems could bring water to potential grazing grounds where there is grass but no drinking water. In South Africa, there are cattle which obtain their liquid from gourds, and expect to chew water when they come upon a stream. The tying up of cattle to a money economy among the Ankole, too, would ease pressure on grazing ground.

The cultural problems involved can likewise be solved. They would largely concern attitudes to land. Sometimes individual tenure of land is favourably contrasted with communal rights in land. It is said that the latter hold hazards for any private development of land, while individual tenure, it is further said, stimulates long-term development of land. A man, it is said, is more likely to borrow money to develop land that he owns than land in which he merely has a permissive right of use. This may be called the private motor-car theory of development as opposed to an omnibus theory.

The traditional system of land tenure in fact has no great hazards of insecurity, for the allocation of land to families has always been a civic obligation. And use has always established preferential claims. In Northern Rhodesia, where a system of leasehold of land was introduced by the government, holders made the uncertainty of being able to pay rent next year a reason for not doing any extensive work on the land this year. The genuine question is not one of hazards of insecurity, but one of the availability of loans, and the type of loan available. There is an often-fulfilled danger that loans which are obtained from a distant body not directly concerned with agriculture, eg a bank, may be used entirely for other purposes than agricultural ones. The effect of this is that instead of improving his farm and so his income, the farmer has merely anticipated the revenue from his next crop, and has, in fact, pledged it for less than it could fetch, in view of the interest on loans. Many farmers have lost their farms to unscrupulous money-lenders and speculators in this way.

One might say that all administrative lands should be entrusted to central governments as the new paramount power of the area. This, however, exaggerates the debility of the schismatic tendencies of tribal affinities. And, even if achieved, it would make administration impossible and would lead to the most inhuman bureaucracies, especially since communications are in Africa still generally poor. Where the present distribution of land is not equitable, as in Kenya and South Africa, it will be impossible for an African government not to acquire land for more equitable distribution.

The development of farmers' co-operatives could institute an agricultural revolution. It could secure the improvement of agriculture through larger areas of joint and mechanical cultivation. Co-operative methods would also simplify transportation problems, by owning vehicles. A co-operative set-up, making loans available, and supervising their administration could ensure that some at least of the funds provided were spent on improvements. It could possess machinery which it could hire out to farmers more cheaply than the peasant labour for which they have to pay at present. An approach through co-operatives would certainly prevent the further growth of a wealthy land-owning class with a debt-encumbered, rent-paying vortex.

In East and South Africa, it will be necessary for an African government to acquire land for equitable redistribution. When a government does this, naturally, it will have to compensate owners for the improvements to the land. When through nearby public development, however, a private site acquires enhanced value, this arbitrary increase in value should not be taken account of by a purchasing government. In African traditional systems, one recalls that when a party is aggrieved through theft or injury, the compensation to which he is entitled is allowed to include any reasonable gains that might have accrued to him, and of which he now stands deprived, between the commission of the act and the settlement of the action. This provision does not, however, allow for calculations future to the settlement. Hence, since any increase in the value of a private site, due to neighbouring development at public expense, can only be reasonably based on future calculations, the traditional African equity does not allow for such increases in value to be made available to the private holder in arrangements for compensation.

The resources for manufacturing industrialisation are most bright. The tinplate of the world is boiled in African palm-oil. Mass-production techniques have profited greatly from African cobalt, once indispensable for making high-speed tool steel. Apart from Soviet sources, the Congo and Canada are the only worthwhile areas in the world for cobalt. The largest known deposits of copper lie in Africa, in the copper plateaux of Katanga and Northern Rhodesia. The radium of the Congo represents sixty per cent of the West's sources. There is plenty of gold in South Africa and Ghana. African diamonds are among the largest ever found. Ghana and Sierra Leone have an abundance of industrial diamonds. Africa produces one-third of the world's chrome ore and vanadium, and one-fifth of the world's manganese. Ghana is practically made of manganese and bauxite. Africa has no shortage of iron, which is to be found in Southern Sudan and the East African mountains. Africa has some coal and some oil. There is no continent better endowed by nature with natural resources than Africa. The two things that Africa lacks are skill and capital; for both are needed to convert natural resources into finished products. If Africa counts her resources continentally, then she has a unified culture, an advantageous population, energy, mineral deposits, agricultural promise, and international goodwill within limits. Like the Soviet Union and America, Africa has internally nearly all the raw materials she could need for manufacturing industries.

As to the shortage of capital, Africa can reduce the seriousness of this through improved agriculture. Africa's under-population appears here as an economic asset, for it points at agricultural industrialisation as a means of economic improvement. Denmark and New Zealand, for example, have economies almost entirely agricultural and their under-population has been an asset in building up such an economy, for it made it easier to amass surpluses for export. Indeed, one advantage of an agricultural industry is that the skills involved are simpler and more easily attained compared to those involved in the general run of manufacturing industries. And agricultural produce is always sold more easily than manufactured goods.

There are other measures of great vigour which Africa must take if the serious shortage of capital is to be remedied. Steps must be taken to ensure that less of the capital owned in Africa is locked up in foreign banks. Africa must have banks of a continental size to make up for the shortcomings in intensity of activity by the added resources of extensive activities. In the operation of the foreign banks in Africa, a limited amount of the money collected is kept locally in the banks as imprest, but the greater bulk is transmitted to Europe. The correction of this anomaly should be in the establishment of state banks and co-operative banks.

Savings should be encouraged in African banks, as long as care is taken to neutralise the restrictive effect of savings on investment; as long as one saves one's money, one is not investing it. It is true, however, that state and co-operative banks can make the proceeds of savings available in loans to businesses.

The control of profits is another measure that could be taken to assist capital formation. As long as profits accrued in Africa are exported outside Africa for use outside Africa, profits have a proportionate retardation on the growth of capital. Wages too must be related to productivity and wherever productivity is not optimum wages should not be subsidised to the detriment of capital growth. In certain cases, it will of course be impossible to assess the productivity of labour. The civil service, political office, and academic service are three areas which offer examples of the impossibility of sensibly defining and measuring productivity. And while touching on productivity, one must say that the African family organisation does not in any way lower productivity.

To complete examples of the ways in which capital could be built, Africa must not be too shy to borrow. Foreign capital mixed with African management must be invited with protective guarantees to quicken the African acquisition of skills.

African centres of distribution should be created to handle some of the consumer imports from Europe. It has been said that European manufacturers have refused in the past to divert some of their exports to African agents, showing an unmistakable preference for European agents in Africa. But this kind of monopolistic preference could be broken. If one took motor-cars as an example, African distributing bodies could be formed with governmental guarantees, who could negotiate with individual manufacturers in any of a number of countries for distribution of a particular brand of car. If the British Motor Corporation, for example, should feel unable to conclude such negotiations, the French Renault organisation, or the German Volkswagen organisation, or Russian or Italian small car concerns could be approached and naturally one or other would be ready to play cricket. In this way some of the profits entailed in motor-car distribution would be kept in Africa for capital use. It would be dangerous to use this method in a wholesale way for all consumer imports for it would cut down on efficiency in distribution and might encourage monopolistic evils. It could, however, be successfully used in the case of isolated types of manufactured goods.

In studying the political problems of Africa, one has to look at the types of political organisations which have grown in Africa, for it is by these organisations that political problems will be solved, and indeed it is in terms of their patterns that problems will be recognised and formulated. At bottom, however, there are two problems in national politics. There is the problem of power, and there is the problem of unity: the problem of how one sub-group of a nation or territory shall acquire executive and legislative predominance, and the problem of how to maintain the allegiance of the people or, at least, preserve their acquiescence. In Africa, the first problem has preoccupied political organisations more than the second. This is the habit of nationalist movements. Inevitably, they impose a hegemony, a hegemony of élite and a hegemony of policy. Thus, it comes to be that the now customary contrast between patron parties and mass parties no longer centres on the possession or otherwise of an élite but almost exclusively on their method of organisation.

Today in Africa, mass parties are without doubt predominant. A few years ago, with the backing of the French administration it seemed that patron parties would swamp what was then French Africa. But with the triumph of the *Parti Democratique de la Côte d'Ivoire* of Ivory Coast, the age of patron parties in French Africa came to a neat end. Patron parties may be so called because they are organised around influential and prestigious personalities, and obtain the loyalty of their following not through any direct appeals to them but through the *charisma* of the names of regional personalities and the loyalties that this *charisma* invokes. But because patron parties neglect the details of manifestoes through which, Vicar of Bray-like,

THE MIND OF AFRICA

each region and locality can be pacified and ravished, and their consolidation at branch level maintained, this neglect seriously affects their stability; for with the cooling-off of a nuclear personality, the vortex which he trails into a patron party also gets dissipated. Discussion at moments of crisis becomes irrational, and turns more on the fulminations of scandalised dignitaries than on logical pros and cons. The behaviour of their local following becomes truly hysterical. At this point, the patron party exhibits one of its paradoxes, its lack of disciplined cohesion compared with mass parties, and a tendency towards fragmented hysteria. The personalities around which patron parties have gathered in Africa are naturally enough those of chiefs and successful businessmen. Examples of patron parties may be said to be the *Union Nigerienne des Independants et Sympathisants* of Niger, and the Northern People's Congress of Nigeria. Ethnic parties, because they readily blot up the hierarchic sentiments of tribal structures, can also be designated as patron parties. An example of an ethnic party is the *Parti de Solidarite Senegalaise*, which belongs to rural personalities. The dangers of tribalism in the larger groupings, more than ever before to be found today in Africa, could be serious, and they arise mainly from the organisation of ethnic affinities into political forces. The success of these political forces comes to be interpreted as the triumph of a particular ethnic grouping, and schismatic tendencies endemic in the *pasticio* nations of Africa become excited. The areas where ethnic parties are really serious are Kenya, Uganda, and the ex-Belgian Congo. These are areas where such parties have not succeeded in controlling decisive majorities. In the Federation of Nigeria, where parties are associated with ethnic groupings, regionally such parties have amassed near-total majorities, hence the presence of minor ethnic groupings constitutes no problems for regional unity. The Action Group is associated with the Yoruba peoples of Western Nigeria, and the presence of a few Ibo-speaking persons in Western Nigeria who support the National Council of Nigeria and the Cameroons, which is associated with the Ibo peoples, does not normally call forth a cold sweat in the Action Group. Not all ethnic parties are patron parties, and both The

National Council of Nigeria and the Cameroons and the Action Group, its chiefly leadership notwithstanding, are mass parties.

It could be said of patron parties that the inter-connection between their branches is grossly weak, their articulation is poor; compared to mass parties, they are defective in discipline and they have very little direct membership participation, thriving more on supporters than on members. The personal nature of the leadership of patron parties sometimes conflicts with the proliferation of personalities at the local level. Open quarrels and breaches consequently occur more readily. Sometimes these occur between some local bigwig and the national leader and then the effect is for a splinter group to emerge. Sometimes too there is bickering between minor bigwigs, and then the main effect is one of lassitude following active vituperation. In the latter kind of case, the leaders of the patron party add to their decision-making function one of reconciliation of conflict. The very absence of a disciplined and formalistic internal cohesion in a patron party holds a considerable fascination for chiefly elements. The disorganisation of such a party bars any effect from being transmitted from its lower reaches to the patrons of the party echelon. The only public to whose opinion it is responsive consist of its leaders, nor does it normally formulate policies in terms of the immediate mass good. The chief, espying a chance to reassert his traditional but fast-dwindling leadership, espouses the cause of the patron party. The patron party is then admired by the colonial administration as representing the true disposition of the people. The conservative deadweight which the chief brings into the patron party in an attempt to save his traditional dignity warms the heart of the colonial administration. Earlier on, however, most patron parties were dislodged by mass parties. Those in Mali and Guinea were defeated in 1956 by the *Union Soudanaise* and the *Parti Demicratique de Guinée*, both of them mass parties. In countries with effective patron parties parallel struggles were carried on. The main struggle was, of course, against political dependence. In this, the chiefly element in the patron party attempted to reassert its claim to political position in its own territory. At the same time the mass elements in the patron parties joined issue with the leadership by patronage. The recovery of political independence is seen by mass elements not as the return of historical conditions but as a revolution, not as a cyclic achievement but as a linear leap. In such a struggle between patron elements and mass elements, the issue is bound to be resolved in favour of mass elements. In Africa today, patron elements are too vulnerable, for they offer caution, restraint, class-consciousness, to the masses of the people, whereas mass leaders can make optimistic promises to their elements, excite an upsurge of will and a renewed sense of power in them, and offer intimations of the good life of plenty and leisure. The promises of mass leaders guide their hands to socialistic devices. In Niger, Sawaba and in Northern Nigeria, National Council of Nigeria and the Cameroons, parties with mass complexions, have not yet resolved the struggle to their satisfaction.

Examples of victorious mass parties are the *Parti Democratique de Guinée*, the Convention People's Party of Ghana, the *Union Soudanaise* of Mali, the *Parti Democratique de la Côte d'Ivoire* of the Ivory Coast, the Action Group of Nigeria and the National Council of Nigeria and the Cameroons, also of Nigeria. Of these, the Convention People's Party of Ghana rests on a paid-up membership of two millions and a half out of a total national population of seven million. The mass party characteristically claims to represent all the people. The bases of this claim are various. The Action Group of Nigeria, for the sake of an example, was earlier on very closely articulated, rigorously disciplined, and its members could directly initiate and influence policy. Its membership had little inertia, it had a power of self-movement. The *Parti Democratique de Guinée* was another example. The *Union Soudanaise* was a third. On account of these features they claimed, not unreasonably, to represent the national will. This claim was an arithmetical claim, its verification was direct, through observation, and counting after argument. There was another type of basis, however, which had nothing to do with the *enumeratio simplex*. Here the claim to represent all the people and to embody the national will was based on ideas about the missionary nature of the mass party. Here the emphasis is on the leadership of the party, not on its following. In this way, an approximation is initiated to the patron party. The leadership of the party enters claims about its grasp, antecedent to enquiry, of the interests of the people, formulates these interests for the people, and in the name of the people pursues the interests of the people formulated for the people. There grows a tendency to regard the people and the state as a supra-individual, a sort of epiphenomenon, awesome, primeval, and, if one may say so, blubberous. In the long run, however, little practical difference survives between the two mass party attitudes. Mass parties mould themselves in time into the second cast of mind, of which communist parties are the most striking examples. Communist parties resemble patron parties in being very narrowly based in direct membership, and resemble mass parties in their perfect articulation and discipline. The hegemony of their leadership is, however, as complete as only that of a patron party can be. The revolutionary fervour which carries the mass party to political independence, animated by the desire to restore power not merely to the territory, but to the people, is a double revolution. It is both a revolution against the colonial administration and a revolution against the traditional chiefly hegemony. With the gaining of political independence, the mass party assumes the leadership of the nation, and it is thus that the mesmerism of the name of the people begins. To complete the mesmerism of this name, power, and so leadership, comes to be concentrated in the hands of a new political élite. The fewer the people who are enabled to initiate policies in the name of the people for all the people, the greater is the apparence of the constraining power of that name, an almost magical name, a Cratylean name.

But this assumption of the rights and abilities of a people into new hands could easily lead to horrific brutalities. No individual, it comes to be said, is greater than the people. Hence all the people, albeit not together but individually, but still all, are gently lowered in worth by the miracle of their own compound name. The fact that the people comprise persons shimmers away into the inaccessible reaches of mysticism. In Africa, however, a great deal that is indigenous in tradition, if kept in mind, could preserve the people from the dangers of a hardened revolution. Already, Africa is in a position to seize the dilemma by one horn. The future of Africa depends on a number of parallel revolutions. The past of Africa can authenticate the revolutions. The egalitarian and humane mentality of traditional African social organisation can yield principles in terms of which not only aims, but means also, can be judged and authenticated. There must be aims which are African in the sense that they stand authenticated and even recommended by African traditions: there must be means which are African in the same sense. Some ways of doing things can be shown in this sense to be African ways of doing things. The success of revolutions depends not merely on the glorification of their objectives but, centrally, on the avenues of pursuit.

The revolutionary ideals of mass parties have everything to do with the size of their following. But their size cannot be explained adequately by the piquancy of their ideals alone. The breadth of the mass party's appeal is paralleled by the diversity of its sub-organisations. It has women's and youth organisations, it is associated with trade unions and publishes its own newspapers. In farming out its activities it combines a thesis, an antithesis, and a synthesis. In its narrow concern as a political party, it represents a synthesis, a reconciliation by tempering and elimination of multifarious interests, urges, and drives; in its ancillary activities, it nourishes the same sectional interests and strengthens the same narrower unities and loyalties, as it were recreating its thesis and antithesis. This is the key to the energy of the mass party in Africa. The opportunities for full participation by its members are comprehensive.

Mass parties, even when they begin by being revolutionary, appear to have a tendency to coalesce responsibility for the revolution in the hands of an emergent élite. The élite, though it is the child of the mass party, soon dissociates itself in spirit and deed, if not in words, from the mass party. It becomes increasingly difficult to see in the private activities of its members a true reflection of the revolutionary ideals which should animate them. The ideals of a mass party which grows up in conditions of public and private poverty, disease, and ignorance and hunger, cannot avoid being socialistic. The authenticity of mass parties, after they have engendered their own élites, can best be measured by the extent to which the lives and programmes of their élites can be explained in socialistic terms. The people who form the new élite of the mass party are not necessarily the people who under the colonial administration were most crucially affected emotionally by racial, cultural, social or professional discrimination, people who were painfully affected by such discrimination because they did not have the inabilities which such discrimination implied, and were in fact capable of enjoying and profiting from the freedoms denied them. Such men sometimes came to resent the exploitation of their people and the casual attitude to their destiny which the colonial powers had. Their resentment was heightened by the exclusion which they themselves suffered. Sometimes, however, persons like these survived in the élite of the mass party. In their revolutionary days there was in them a pious yearning for justice on a large scale which translated itself into socialist tendencies, socialism offering the most meaningful way in which such justice on a large scale could be most speedily formulated and expressed. In a few cases, members of the élite have allowed this casuistic yearning to be corrupted into narrower ambitions. This corruption of ideals was not, however, an aspect of independence movements.

This debilitating of ideals might be understood in terms of the weakening in the direct mass participation, when an alternative, differently inspired machinery is set up. When such a machinery has been set up, party congresses become fewer or even disappear altogether.

Nevertheless, there are psychological conditions of this weakening in the ideals of the mass party. When this has happened in the past there were, firstly, differences in the level of education inside the élite. Hence, if education were made to matter, the exalted equality of the élite might be imperilled. Secondly, there were also differences of generation—especially among the Senegalese leaders of the *Bloc Democratique*, the leaders of the Senegalese Federation of the *Section Française de l'Internationale Ouvrière*. This difference in generation was the seam at which the old United Gold Coast Convention burst, with the younger members collecting around the off-shoot, the CPP. Finally, there were also differences of ideology. These differences were not often explicit enough to be ideological. When they were neither complex nor articulate, they might be said to be differences in taste rather than in ideology. The programmes of the *Parti Democratique de Guinée* and the *Union Soudanaise* were avowedly Marxist-inspired. The official statements of the *Union Progressiste Senegalaise* are Catholic-Socialist under the scholastic guidance of Senghor. The *Parti du Regroupement Africain* would, one supposes, be called Trotskyist. It would be a mistake to visit all the implications of Marxism, or Catholic-Socialism, or Trotskyism on these African parties. They have not quite worked out their blueprint for paradise yet, and they certainly do not accept those implications which may in a theoretical way be gleaned from the appellations that they do not reject.

To make these differences ineffectual, individuals of the élite had to direct their efforts towards more personal ends. And an attempt was made to preserve the egalitarianism of the élite by its members looking after themselves and their own.

Though the mass party tends to lose some of its socialistic fervour in this way, it has really fulfilled significant roles in Africa. In the first place, it was responsive to its public opinion, but although in a way it continues to be responsive to public opinion, the public whose opinion it still responds to contracts greatly. The mass party has also satisfied 'identity quests' in Africa The 'identity quest' is equally a result of the British and the French methods of administration in Africa. British forces in Africa were very thin on the ground, and the areas for which Britain was responsible totalled some four million square miles. Such small forces, especially where communications were poor, could do little to restore order should it be really disturbed over wide areas. To make up for this deficiency, Britain refrained from disturbing the traditional set-up as much as possible, relying on the authority of local chiefs; she governed and kept order through these local chiefs. Consequently, the patriotism of the peoples was never really transferred to Britain. With the crumbling of the chiefs in what was British Africa, during the brief agitation for independence, and with the preserved integrity of traditional forces through Britain's indirect rule, the people—who were now identified not as a number of distinct tribes, but as a self-conscious country—became restive, and the peripheries of their identity and unity began to melt into the new larger context. The pressure which this involved led them to seek new nation-wide identities. Though the French in contrast undermined the authority of the chiefs and attempted to bring up their colonial subjects to look towards France, this re-orientation was confined to the educated few. The general run of Colonials became even more restive than their British counterparts, and they adhered to trade unions and political parties with a comparable readiness and assiduity.

The theory of the clan, it has been seen, assigned people to tribes and clans before they were born on the strength of the origins of their spiritual factors. Identity at this level was something that one could not shake off or lose. This idea that because of ante-natal spiritual factors, a living individual had an ante-natal identity, encouraged questions of identity to become central in Africa. Questions about ante-natal identity, family identity, clan identity, tribal identity, all became central to human activity, and also to the analysis of human actions. The authorship of actions became more interesting than the classification of the act. Indeed, the authorship was held to throw light on the classification of the act. Not indifferently, what might in a general way be called the same act was punished or not, according to who did it. Nor was this an expression of partiality or favouritism. Moral epithets attached first and foremost to agents and only derivatively to their actions. Actions were therefore usually classified according to the intentions which one found it natural to attribute to the agents, who differed in character. Their characters were not an effulgence of their acts. Their acts rather, had their spring and source in character.

This preoccupation with identity has not been abruptly ended by the loosening of the traditional structure. It is part of the explanation of the success of trade union organisations and political parties, their strong militancy in Africa having been a source of the feeling of committal, identity, and loyalty. This is the new 'belonging'.

The all-embracing nature of African trade unions and political parties imbues them with a socialistic strain. Whereas socialism has been a corrective in Europe and America, it has been the pristine condition in Africa in the form of communalism as described earlier. Socialism is an endeavour to restrict socio-political significance to those differences which are biological for the species of the nation. Class differences in traditional African socialism therefore tended to be purely aesthetic and for the sake of pageant. The Akan saying that all men are children of God and none is a child of earth, was taken seriously in Africa, and it was a guiding principle in socio-political arrangements. It is not that the communal African society was pleasantly homogenised. Differences among men were, of course, recognised, but these differences were not allowed to make a difference in certain spheres. African socialism was intensely humanistic. It was not a narrow economic doctrine, but a socio-political one. Each was responsible for all, and all were responsible for each. Socialism is ethical, and is directed alike towards equality, freedom, and fellowship. In the new African contexts, socialism cannot be left to the force of religious ardour, but must now be organised at government level. The *laissez-faire* private socialism of the untechnical society cannot serve any more, for the introduction of new techniques into Africa has imbalanced the likely quantities which individuals left to their own devices could privately amass. Centralised socialism is the only way of continuing to ensure that each individual attains a certain minimum of goods and services.

Sooner or later, one wishes to know what room is left for individual freedom in all this.

One must admit that every society has its own forms of terrorism. In some societies, these forms are more subtle and even indsidious than in others. Even a free and democratic society invents its own perfect instruments of terrorism, be it the sermon in the pulpit, the tyranny of trade unions, the conformism of the political party, or the scarification by

Government and Opposition Whips, the opprobrium inflicted by the press, the ridicule of friends or the ostracism of colleagues; the sneer, the meaningful elevation of the eybrows, the tightening or pursing of the lips, the setting of the shoulder and poising of the chin preparatory to the administration of the snub; or countless other devices. Terrorism is, of course, always obnoxious, and rather effective in ensuring that individual behaviour does not become too bizarre, that freedom does not degenerate into excessively outlandish eccentricity. The individual is not an anarchic unit. He lives in orderly surroundings, and the effecting of the orderliness of his surroundings calls for a degree of subjection and regimentation, where education has not inculcated the desired responses. When this subjection and regimentation is subtle, as it is in free and democratic societies, it represents the kid glove which muffles up the iron fist. The gentilities of democratic terrorism could often become a cloak for cruelty and selfishness. But the terrorisms of a free and democratic society are, of course, the most humane in the world, for even if the individual is defeated, he is at every point accorded a fighting chance.

One way of looking at under-developed countries, however, is to see them as being in a perpetual state of siege. Western political theory too has incorporated in it the idea that at critical stages of siege or an emergency of one kind or another the political structure of a country undergoes legitimate alteration of a limited and temporary nature. Certain liberties or rights may be temporarily restricted or drawn differently. Countries in the state of parallel and rapid fundamental development might be said to be in this situation for a certain period of time. Crises call for extraordinary measures. An under-developed country today faces all its problems at the same time; the same problems have faced other countries successively—problems of education, communications, health, food, water, society, economics, unappeased and resurgent tribalism. In some African countries the tribal seams correspond to the political seams in spheres of influence and also to territorial seams inside a federal structure. Such a country, Nigeria for example, is not faced by resurgent tribalism, for because each ethnic cluster is dominant

somewhere, the violence to which protracted frustration gives
way is nipped in the bud.

At the same time governments are not in fact all the same in
their degree of sincerity, even if it is futile to operate on the
assumption that governments are unreasonable. Still, it is only
a government which is entrusted with the right and the power
to declare periods of national crisis. Laws should be passed as
the necessity for them becomes clearer. When a law is prohibitive, it is as if some right were abrogated. What someone
could do in the past that did not constitute an offence, and was
not punishable, comes with the passing of a prohibitive law to
be offensive and punishable. But legislation might in fact be protective of right. Governments in under-developed countries
suffer from tremendous pressures; they are called upon to
regulate rights and reconcile them, to safeguard corporate
rights and interests, and this calls for a sort of qualitative
mathematics, holding this right in abeyance in favour of that
right, or in favour of that profit or gain. But when a government
begins to see itself as the arm, the conscience, the will, and the
prophet of the people, it opens itself to grave temptations, and
is already losing contact with the pulse of the people. But the
mere possibility of the misuse of powers is not itself a criticism.
It is a characteristic feature of achievements that they might
have been corrupted, or might have misfired. Possibility is no
evidence for likelihood. Even a government has just so many
rights. It is bound by its constitution, outside which it cannot
act. Nor can it act against it. In rapidly developing countries,
where cultures have been slapped on to cultures, and everything
is fluid, forms with strong outlines have to be secured.

The role of intellectuals in such situations becomes critical.
Intellectuals in under-developed or rapidly developing countries
are subject to two kinds of pull—first, the pull which all
intellectuals share, the pull involved in the notion that in-
tellectualism is universal, and not national. Second, they are
subject to the pull of the demands of whatever nation they
belong to. To the extent that they yield to this second pull
they may be said to be national or nationalistic intellectuals.
This duality in the pulls to which they are subject creates a

possible conflict in their role. One might find some intellectuals, for example, emphasising the universal aspect of their qualities and some other intellectuals emphasising the nationalistic aspects of their qualities, especially the latter case, when their nation is rapidly developing or under-developed. Intellectuals in the transient societies are not like the wandering scholars of the European Middle Ages, or like intellectuals in traditional Islam, denationalised, and peripatetic. On the contrary, they are markedly tied to their countries even if one takes account of those who, nearer to the Middle Ages tradition, seek and obtain employment with the United Nations Organisation. The common picture is not one of Asian and African intellectuals moving from one country to another—being journalists in one place, cabinet ministers in another and then finishing up, perhaps, as historians in a third. On the whole their careers depend on identification with particular regions. Their internationalism is rather that which is involved in following up one's academic training, involved, for example, in their continuing to be philosophers or experts on Shakespearean texts, at a time when their nation, because it is transient or because it is rapidly developing, could also appreciate their prowess at endeavours of, perhaps, more immediate consequence. They must be distinguished from intellectuals in anchored societies who either fulfil a role which their society needs, like the priesthood in Ancient Egypt, or who pursue their academic studies in a national condition in which there is no marked shortage of technologists, civil servants, *et cetera*. The intellectuals of Western Europe and America, as well as of the Soviet Union, are not technicians, but rather people who are able to become technicians, who form a kind of pool upon which their country can draw in times of stress, as when, during the last war, university teachers became engaged in highly specialised functions which were at the same time quite different from their training and professional pursuits. This kind of versatility is a consequence of the quality rather than the direction of their own professional pursuits. Intellectuals are indispensable to any objective community.

In under-developed societies, however, it is a pity when

intellectuals become tired intellectuals. An intellectual has become tired when the possibility of new ideas, fulgurating with excitement, escapes him. The intellectual is a kind of expert, and an expert is someone from whom ideas seem to come with ease. This means, naturally, that intellectuals tend to lean on their memory and habits, on what they have worked out and are used to. Nevertheless only intellectuals can be socially sensitive to the possibilities and dangers affiliated to rapid development with a minimum of waste and great economy. In rapidly developing countries, they are even more useful than elsewhere.

Any society depends for its survival on a marked measure of objectivity, and the critical and unemotional apparatus which the intellectual is able to bring to the examination of questions and problems is always valuable. Constructive discussion is geared to objectivity.

The foreign policy of Africa might be broken into two parts: a foreign policy as regards Africa herself, and directed towards increasing unity in that continent, and, as regards the rest of the world, a foreign policy based on a studious neutralism. As regards Africa, one might say that the future of the African continent can be brightest if the unity of the continent is achieved. As long as Africa remains divided not merely territorially, but in such a way that there is prestigious rivalry, even hostility, between country and country, that continent will not have the strength and importance which its size and natural wealth ought to give it. Africa is probably the richest continent in the world. Like the Soviet Union and continental America, it certainly has inside itself all that it could need for its industrial development, barring skill and capital.

Neutralism is not a perverse refusal to choose between good and evil. Neutralism has nothing at all to do with such a choice. The irritations between capitalism and communism, which seem to be brewing into a storm already, are not felt so keenly by neutral countries because the involvement and fundamental commitment responsible for the irritations have not been experienced by them. Communism and capitalism are, *in situ*, certainly not seen in mitigated terms of black and white. Neutral countries are somewhat reluctant to take postures in advance of questions, such that the reply to a question is already given even before the question is asked. They prefer to look at questions as they arise and form opinions upon them on their merits. Neutralism is freedom from prejudice, it is not a reluctance to make judgments. This alone is valuable in the antithetic stance of communism and capitalism. The fact that there are unformed opinions and judgments helps in preventing the two systems from really meeting. Neutral countries form a sort of buffer, a shock-absorber, between them. They are the occasion of a moderating influence on the two systems. For their sake, the protagonists of the systems are willing at times to seem reasonable. The opinions of neutrals, which need not be the same, will inevitably go against one side now, now against the other. When these opinions hold little comfort for one side on some specific issue, it is not to be thought that this is symptomatic of a submerged general hostility. Neutralism is the denial of such general feelings. Its opinions are symptomatic of nothing.

It must be remembered that there are a few neutralist bodies in the world today. The British Commonwealth is an example. The Commonwealth is a neutral body. Some of its members are also members of some by no means neutral alliances. The neutralism of the Commonwealth ensures that it is not an aggressive union, but a progressive one. Commonwealth countries which are not members of committed alliances are able to interpret, with credibility and sympathy, the attitudes and points of view of non-neutral members of the Commonwealth to those to whom they are opposed. But its variegated composition is part of the strength of the Commonwealth. Internally the Commonwealth is strong, because it represents a multiple diversity. There would be little value in a club where everyone enjoyed the same opinions on the same topics. There would be altogether lacking that enrichment of the personality and the intellect which results from appreciating alternative points of view. The illumination of one's problems which can arise from seeing similar problems differently interpreted and approached with different attitudes of mind is something for which every Commonwealth country should be thankful. The state is nowadays not such an internally oriented organism as it once was. Of the state as an internally oriented organism, America before the First World War and after, and Japan, much earlier on, have perhaps presented the most startling examples in modern times. Today, the influence of international relations on the alignment of forces inside the nation itself is considerable. What one country will consider to be admissible inside itself is increasingly being critically affected by international relations. Every country has some measures and arrangements which it cannot put into effect for fear of being compromised in the eyes of others whose good opinion and co-operation it desires and cherishes. In one way, this is a sign of some degree of international unity. Unfortunately, it follows patterns which have made the resulting divisions almost intractable. For instance, though NATO and the Warsaw Pact could be held up as examples of international unity, they follow patterns which make the divisions between NATO and the Warsaw Pact intractable.

If the Commonwealth is strong inside itself, outside too it is strong. Its external strength will depend on the extent to which it is not narrow, restricted, and dogmatic. To point the way to international unity in amity, it must show both that it contains differences, and that it can survive them. A narrowly uniform group cannot point the way of unity to a world which is irreducibly diverse. The Commonwealth must show that though its members are diverse not only in race, but also in outlook, experience, and programme, it does not feel disrupted and can still recognise abiding areas of co-operation in equality.

Africa is faced with a number of parallel revolutions. It is faced with political, economic, communicational, and educational revolutions, and with others of similar kinds. In these revolutions, elements of solidity and boon in the traditional heritage should be watched over, and not permitted to be carried away in the revolutionary cascade as sad flotsam surviving from a pre-modern age. Africa needs a constant reminder of its massively traditional nature. And its best prospects lie in utilising this tradition and heritage.

There is a great deal in the ethics of Africa, for example, which is passionately humanistic. And the revolutions of Africa must not be allowed to swamp Africa's own humanist ethics. Even revolution needs an ethical justification. There are in Africa today certain practices which, though never problematic in African traditional ethics, have, however, irritated the European morality to such an extent indeed that not a few Africans themselves pose the questions now as moral issues. Chief of these is the issue of polygamy. Africa is still polygamous. The attainment of education has not in Africa always induced a loathing for, or condemnation of, polygamy. In Moslem Africa, and also, though less frequently, in Christian areas, polygamy is still practised by persons of notable educational attainments, even when they have been brought into touch with Christian ethics. Polygamy is an extensive social fact and deserves to be treated with the utmost seriousness.

Is polygamy immoral? When, with intimations of rhetoric, monogamy is held up as the only complete form of marriage, a true partnership between two beings, a man and a woman, in all senses, not merely in an economic one, not merely in the sense of looking after and producing a family, but in the sense above all of companionship—to the exclusion of all others—when all this is said, it must be suggested that marriage has a sociology also. In Africa, it has been found that polygamy has been widespread mostly in areas where infant mortality is high, where sterility is rampant, and females greatly outnumber males, and also sometimes, where a plurality of wives is prestigious. These are not insignificant correlations and can be brought to bear on ethical discussions about contraception.

No, the merits of polygamy ought to be weighed against those of monogamy. In Eastern Nigeria, polygamy is actually encouraged by the women, and they manage to live quite often in harmony and without animosity. Polygamy and monogamy as systems of marriage seem to have a connection with ideas about the foundation of society. Where society is thought to be based on individual rights, the tendency is towards monogamy, because one holds that the rights of an individual should not be encroached upon. And a monogamous system of marriage tends to conserve this position. If one on the other hand holds society to be founded on a network of duties and obligations, then the fact that an individual's right to food might have to be limited because there is an extra mouth to feed, would not weigh heavily. Illegitimate children as well as legitimate ones are equally members of the same society, and when one is actuated primarily by one's obligation to members of society, illegitimacy as a differentiation of the rights of children becomes non-existent, and polygamy has no excoriating effect on individual rights.

Where the economic life of a people is an acquisitive rather than a communalistic one, it is natural that women should prefer monogamy. In the Islamic communities of Egypt, Tunisia and Algeria, where women are able to become clerks and teachers in large numbers, the movement towards restricting polygamy has considerable force. In Tunisia, polygamy has been abolished, notwithstanding the fact that Islamic law permits it. Where economic life is communalistic, the communalism also seeks expression in polygamous attachments. African societies have in fact already become partially industrialised and also partially acquisitive. And a number of men and women show little inclination towards polygamy.

But, once more, is polygamy immoral?

If it is, it is at least clear that it cannot be the partnership aspect of marriage which makes polygamy immoral. Many partnerships are polypartnership. Even companionship and friendship do not require to be restricted to two persons to be successful. If getting married once is not immoral, getting married twice cannot be immoral.

It must nevertheless be admitted that the preference, certainly the longing of women, is for monogamy. Monogamy implies the acquisition of new sensibilities, a readiness to attain an integrated discipline, an offering of the self in service and sacrifice, a closed communion. One might even say it is a delightful prejudice. It is always an ideal.

Education in Africa must equip Africans with the personality-resources for meeting and coping with the intensities of the African situation. The confusion at the end of the period of the loss of independence is due to the fact that there has never been a value vacuum in Africa. Value conflict in educated Africans, in the attempt to strike a satisfying balance between individual exclusiveness and responsibilities to one's relations, is a reflection of such a confusion. The attitudes which migrants bring to urban areas, being traditional ones, introduce their own patterns of strain in urban surroundings. The peculiarities of this strain are another expression of the confusion. Strain is a reaction, hence the bare experience of others elsewhere is not to be assumed without enquiry to be a guide. There are proved differences in the psychological and cultural complex of attitudes, beliefs, values, emotional discipline, on which urbanity reacts in Africa and in Europe. At no period has Europe been in the present situation of Africa. Europe has never been confronted in its history by a continent that stood to it as Europe stands today to Africa. There are social problems which have to be understood and solved. There are also questions of national development, of health, communications, education, industry. Education in Africa must enable as many as possible to understand the strains and stresses to which the continent is subjected, to appreciate the changes that take place, to contribute fully in a true socialist spirit for the benefit of all. If education is linked with the solution of problems, then it is just as well to recognise that there are different types of problems. It cannot, for example, be that all the problems that face any nation at any time are purely vocational in character. Many of a nation's problems touch on liberalism, concern human values, and policies directly affecting human beings. These problems, however they might be illumined by quantitative terms, cannot without residue be formulated in such terms. And the sensitivity of mind and spirit required for weighing relevant considerations here is attained and sharpened otherwise than through a vocational training. At any time there will be some needs of the nation which are urgent. Urgent needs are by definition contemporary needs. But the educational structure of a nation should not be rigidly geared in an *ad hoc* and opportunist way to problems of the day alone. Education is a perennial activity, and who can tell what the needs of a nation will be from time to time, who can tell how they might change? Needs change, some are satisfied, some fall into abeyance, and new ones arise or are created. The educational structure of a nation should be primed to make remedial provisions for changing and even unforeseen needs. The ability to do this is an explanation of that seeming lack of realism which troubles so many universities. The readiness to tackle problems which have not arisen and might not even be described, could, when matched against urgent and excruciating problems, shimmer with fantasy. A plea must be made in the new nations of Africa for sympathy and understanding of the virtues of this fantasy. It would be wrong, however, for a university to smother, dope itself, with the pleasures of this, for when a university becomes an impervious ivory tower, unresponsive to the problems of the present because of a seer-like preoccupation with those of the past and of the future, it becomes somewhat implausible.

The educational structure of a nation can be given a contemporary emphasis and orientation at certain points in standard ways. For example, scholarships in certain branches of learning can be made more plentiful than in others, for the period during which the shortage of qualified persons in the former is acute. Departments can be enlarged to respond to pressures or demand of skill. It must be remembered that in many cases the value of a learned man to his community is not in what he has learnt or the use to which he might be able to put it, but rather in the disciplined habits of mind, the sharpening and energising of brain-power entailed in his seemingly irrelevant scholastic odyssey.

Education in Africa has not in fact had much flexibility in the past. It was geared exclusively to what were regarded in a painfully narrow-minded way as the problems of the day. These seem to have consisted in the urgency for clerks and catechists. The result is that a grotesque imbalance has been generated in African education today. Through the efforts of national governments this imbalance is being slowly removed.

The genesis of this imbalance is connected with the early egocentric standpoint of European studies of Africa. Africa was not to Europeans a continent with its own integrity.

Education was therefore devised not to serve African societies and at the same time preserve the harmony of society; it was devised to strengthen the service of Africa to Europe. It was therefore given an austere shape and a minimal content.

Their early anthropologists too suffered from the same egocentrism in their assumption that African societies were less successful versions of theirs, that African religious and metaphysical beliefs were poor scientific speculations. This assumption was made natural, but no less mistaken, by the intellectual *milieu* from which the anthropologists sprang. Living in the scientific age in Europe, they mused that all other societies had similar concerns to theirs but were only lacking in prowess. When they had to ponder about ancient Greek societies, they were readier, because these were not contemporary with their own society, to treat Greek views as philosophical or metaphysical rather than scientific in the main. But Africa they approached with a parochial form of anthropomorphism. If African governments were themselves prepared to pay money for research into art, religion, and thought, a true and integrated picture of the African personality could easily soon emerge. Social research in Africa and Europe has had an intransigent materialistic basis. In Europe there is more justification for this than in Africa. The grip of materialism on the European mind is more complete than on the African mind. The African mind still responds elementally to art, religion, music, morality; the European mind only as a perfection of sophistication. For a picture of the mind which has a natural sensitivity to these ideas Europe has to delve into its far past. Every now and then one beholds an audience fascinated by Spanish embroidery of the eleventh century. The amount of get up, preparation and education which the modern European mind requires to resuscitate its sense of *rapport* with the beautiful and the sublime, the arid technicalities of his sophistication, is a pointer to his aesthetic desiccation. Educated aestheticism is artificial sensitivity. It is only when sensitivity is natural that it is immediate, effortless, picturesque, non-nostalgic, and intuitive. The sophisticated sensitivity must tear apart what it contemplates. It is an analytic, inquisitive, carving-knife sensitivity. There is a tight hold on that sub-dermal suffusion of myriad tingling feelings, an incipient inebriation which is the quintessence of sensitivity that is sensibility.

But in order that the African's sensitivity should not be lost through an intensely technical education, it is necessary that it should be nurtured through its own local languages. The range of sensitivity is always mirrored in the possibilities of language, and it is through a constant exploitation of these possibilities that the African sensitivity can be best nourished. These possibilities can be exploited first through a documentation of the African traditional literature in order that an accurate consciousness of the languages as recorded languages should be gained. The appreciative familiarity which this makes possible will make it easier for contemporary writers to soak themselves in an autochthonous literary tradition.

In the second chapter, it was indicated that there was a certain identity in the plurality of African traditions and heritage. This identity makes co-operation in methods of preserving the African sensitivity both natural and feasible. Indeed, this is not the only way in which co-operation in Africa can be successful. There are enough identities in that continent to support even pan-Africanism, the ideal of African unity. Enough has been said in Chapter Two to indicate the nature of the cultural identity of Africa. It must always be borne in mind that cultural identity does not imply sameness in the expression of the leading ideas of a culture. We have argued that even a culture that remains the same can vary in *milieux*, as it were, in the face which it turns to the world. In that case, obviously, cultures which are the same can strike different *milieux* at the same time in different places. The institutions and the mannerisms which give expression to a culture depend for their shape and content on prevailing times and local resources. But it is not on these that they depend for their inspiration. Their inspiration arises from philosophical or religious tenets. The identity of the cultures of 'Sudan' Africa consists in the latter.

Objections to pan-Africanism have usually been founded on economic or political matters. It is clear that Africa is united in its interest in economic development. Politicians and statesmen of Africa have said that without economic strength and resilience, political independence is precarious. It might therefore appear to be natural to ask here why one does not seek the integration of Africa through political bonds. Why does one appeal instead to cultural links? The reason is that no area of 'Sudan' Africa is sufficiently developed economically for this to be done significantly. In Europe, most countries are highly developed economically, hence it is possible to integrate Europe without undue hazards for the individual regions of Europe. Indeed the strength of the European economies creates a certain interdependence, a certain inescapable economic contact in trade. Hence there already is an economic bond founded on the acknowledged necessity of rationalising this economic contact. Indeed, the fullness of Africa's cultures is the strength of the cultural argument for pan-Africanism, just as the fullness of Europe's economies is the strength of the economic argument for pan-Europe.

The economies of Africa are not full, strong or resilient. They therefore do not yield the bond which the European economies do.

This does not, however, imply that pan-Africanism is devoid of economic boon for Africa. It is at this point that the objection to it from economic considerations wobbles. Africa is the richest continent in the world. But most of its riches lie stupefied in potentiality and dormancy. Of natural resources, it suffers from an *embarras de richesse*. They are duplicated and reduplicated all over the continent. Though its geological survey is not yet complete, it is already known to contain in scandalous profusion cobalt, copper, radium, uranium, diamonds, vanadium, manganese, chrome ore, bauxite, iron, coal, oil, gold, tin, *et cetera*. A complete geological survey will no doubt reveal further incidences of some of these deposits. Even at the level of raw-material economy, these mineral substances can assist greatly in the formation of capital and the acquisition of wealth in Africa. But need Africa tie itself down to a raw-material economy? What Africa needs to do about its mineral deposits is first to promote an intensive and exhaustive geological survey after the fashion of the Soviet Union. The proof of diverse and plentiful mineral deposits was essential in the confirmation of the

Revolution's success. Indeed, no single state of Africa has the full complement of capital and skill to exploit its resources in the most advantageous way. Capital they might be able to attract externally through loans or investment. Skill they might be able to entice. But if there are large numbers of countries nibbling at the foreign aid which America, Russia, and Europe are disposed to offer, then it is clear that not much will come the way of any individual country. On the other hand, with the example of Great Britain and her seven-million-pound World Bank loan to look to, a united Africa with a composite surplus could ask for and obtain far larger loans than any single African country today can persuade world bodies and other agencies to part with. The larger loans which could become available could more confidently than now be employed in effective exploitation of some of our resources. A united Africa will be able to treat some of its repetitious resources as reserves, and concentrate and streamline effort in the exploitation of them in selected areas. The capital amassed as surplus from such a venture could then be deployed in other areas. Because investment would be rationalised on a continental basis, the rate of growth of the economy of the continent would be far in excess of what it would be otherwise.

Skilled personnel whom industrialised countries can spare are of course limited also, and a united Africa can make better use of them through concentrating them on selected projects than a divided Africa can through dissipating them on competing projects atrophied of care and staff. If Africa unites, of course, there will be problems of currency. Indeed, in the earlier stages it would be unwise to abolish the present currency patterns in favour of an African currency; for one thing, the industrial capacity of Africa to back its own currency will not have been established; for another, a united Africa stands to benefit from the links it will inherit with foreign currencies, thus placing it in a naturally favourable position for purposes of exchange. And the fact that its economy will then be linked with a number of currencies will make it better able to cope with fluctuations in these currencies. Nor need internal trafficking be hampered by this polyvalence in currency. The situation need not be worse than it is today, and the currencies would be interconvertible.

Though Africa is under-developed, its economy is nonetheless heterogeneous. Its economy is uneven. It is pointed out by critics of pan-Africanism that the difference between rich states and poor states, even such as these are in Africa, would be an obstacle not easily to be surmounted. It is said that these discrepancies will account for a certain spontaneous reluctance on the part of richer African regions to throw in their lot too much with that of the poorer regions. Of the British colonies, Ghana is undoubtedly the richest in natural resources, even anticipating Northern Rhodesia. Of the ex-French territories, the Gabon is similarly the richest in natural resources, being most weighted with manganese, uranium and iron around Franceville, Mounana and Nyanga-Chibanga. The ex-Belgian Congo, it is now common knowledge, is also fraught with uranium, copper, and bauxite. Compared to these, many areas of Africa stand denunded both of the favours of God and those of man. But if the indications of the economic benefits of pan-Africanism are correct, then the best course for the richer African states is indeed to throw in their lot with the poorer ones. The sense of brotherhood engendered in the unity of African cultures should make this kind of temporary and enlightened immolation possible and acceptable. The identity of the African cultures, impregnated by a common experience of extra-continental domination and common aspirations, creates a magnetic bond which can be used to bind all regions into a pan-Africa. In a pan-Africa, the African regions can in unison compose their colonial Jeremiad, and also together triumph over it. Already the pattern of inter-African aid is being set. By far the most spectacular example of it is Ghana's placing of ten million pounds at the disposal of Guinea. Nigerians are already talking of aid for Sierra Leone, though in terms of thousands of pounds.

Pan-Africa will be a sort of mutual insurance, economically speaking, for the different regions of Africa. They would practically be guaranteed against total collapse. This kind of insurance would enable them also to rationalise their agriculture. Cocoa is exported in large quantities by Ghana, Nigeria, the Ivory Coast and the Cameroons. A surfeit of it on the world market, thanks to Brazil's unabated contribution, is practically guaranteed. Brazil, with its alternative of coffee, was quite prepared recently, when cocoa prices plunged to tragic depths, to control its marketable volume of cocoa. But African countries, dependent as they were on the revenue from this produce, were quite unable to join Brazil in its proposed adventure. Pan-Africa can diversify and plan its agricultural effort, thus regulating the amount of produce in world markets in order at once to prevent surfeits and obtain the maximum reward for its export effort. Some of the labour so freed can be suitably (and incidentally, quite adequately) employed in the production of food for pan-African consumption. In the same way, palm oil production in Nigeria, the ex-Belgian Congo, and Dahomey can be regulated. Thus, the competitive economies of Africa seem themselves to point at pan-Africanism as a device of optimum leverage.

The underpopulation of Africa is dragged not infrequently like a very dead red herring across the path of African unity. It is only in comparison with other continents that Africa is underpopulated. In terms of its own economic advance, the continent is most clearly not underpopulated. Indeed, its limited population is both an economic and a social benefit. The economic problems which an overpopulated but economically feeble polity has to face are in this way avoided in Africa. The fact there there is only a small number of mouths to feed, compared with India or China, say, means that Africa can quite quickly amass agricultural surpluses, and retain some of its agricultural effort in export activities. The underpopulation of Africa will also hasten the modernisation in technical terms of the continent, for it will create a natural need for mechanisation and automation. In this way, Africans will be enabled to become very rapidly acquainted with technology and be freed in adequate numbers for all types of human and social endeavour consonant with the humanism of their communalism. Here the African's demonstrated speed of learning will tell in his favour. He has already demonstrated his speed of learning in his mastery of European metropolitan languages and sciences.

Rule of thumb and sleight of hand are not likely to present grave difficulties. In two generations, the African has mastered European learning. The pace to which he has thus accustomed himself will carry him over his technological age.

Pan-Africanism finally promises to neutralise the effects of the uneven distribution of population over Africa.

Though pan-Africanism might seem an internal concern of Africa, in its economic and political posture it excites the interest and concern of other continents, especially Europe, with which Africa has up to now been most closely associated. Both Africa and the European Common Market pose problems for each other. The European Common Market depends on the raw materials of Africa and Africa depends on its trade with Europe. But it is most unlikely that the picture which Africa has of its own future is one of a perpetual producer of raw materials for the industries of others. Africa certainly has to sell the raw materials which it cannot use itself. But it has to industrialise, to use more of its own raw materials. A raw-material-producing country which re-imports its materials as finished products inevitably loses because there is absolutely no comparison between the prices which Africa is offered by Europe for its raw materials, and the price which Europe asks of Africa for the finished goods. On balance, therefore, Africa loses considerably. But the Common Market countries would wish to guarantee the sources of their raw materials. It would, therefore, suggest itself to them to retard the industrialisation of Africa as much as they dare. It is essential to Africa that it should not be split by the Common Market. Though the Common Market has little to offer Africa really, it could entrench divisions in that continent through its proposed tariff walls. If the Common Market should stay associated with some but not all African countries which have competing economies, then this is going to prove an added difficulty in the unity of Africa.

It is also sometimes said that the multiplicity of languages in Africa is an effective barrier to pan-Africanism. The Africanist Delafosse distinguished four main language groups in the continent which he identified as the Sudanese, the Nilotic, the semi-Bantu, and the Bantu. Unfortunately his categories have been effectively assailed by the critical acumen of experts like Greenberg who argued that calling any African language semi-Bantu was of the same order of absurdity as calling English semi-German. Westerman, another pundit of African linguistics, invented the piquant expression 'remnant' language for the non-Ewe languages of Togoland. Rather sadly, however, he vouchsafed no clue as to what they were supposed to be remnants of. It is hard on oneself to yield to the guidance of the traditional African linguists. They do not seem to have been sufficiently sensitive to the distinctions between race and economic, occupational, and technological characteristics. George Murdock, for instance, says rightly of the traditionalists that many of them 'appeared to regard the herding and milking of cattle as a linguistic trait and an overriding one at that'. At this point, African linguistics are thrown into an ecstasy. Delafosse, who is often quoted by critics of pan-Africanism who take their standpoint from a putative irreducible lingual babel, is one of those who greatly mixed up categories. He hopelessly substitutes typological for genealogical criteria, surprisingly even at times when he purports to establish genealogical groups. When general and undoubted connections have already been established between typological and genealogical criteria, then it may be methodologically correct to base a conclusion of one type on evidence of the other type. But it is apparently only in Delafosse's mind that doubt about such connections has been sweetly stifled.

When the 'babel' theorists come to avow general similarities among African languages, they tendentiously designate these points of resemblance as connections. It is pointed out that these languages generally employ suffixes, prefixes, and infixes. But so does Greek, for example, in the infixing of *m* in *lambano* from the root *lab*. There is an alleged shortage of vocabulary for abstract terms and a corresponding richness in concrete designations, and in the importance of position to syntax. There are non-African languages of which all these are true. And as to the importance of word order to syntax, this is natural in uninflected languages of which English is an excellent example. Sometimes even where English inflects, but not sufficiently to avoid confusion, word order is still significant to syntax. Consider, for example, the sentences 'Give him her' and 'Give her him'. The explanation of these similarities in Africa through the dynamic expansionism of Islam and commercial relations is not strong enough. A language can only be either inflected in the main or not. Given these two alternatives, and the paucity of other devices to which a language can resort for syntactic purposes (eg word order, tone *et cetera*), it is naïve to see in the mere fact that two languages have similar devices a mystery that calls for theory-spinning.

Whatever one makes of the linguistic palavers, it is clear that the diversity of languages in Africa has not yet made inter-regional contact impossible. Official languages continue to be French and English, Spanish and Portuguese. With these blessings, there is no reason why the pentecostal tongues in Africa should constitute an impediment to unity. The diversity of languages can, so far from being an impediment, indeed by an instrument of unity in the natural interest and effort it creates in the literatures of these languages and so in the qualitative and affective understanding to which such natural interest and effort lead.

Though pan-Africanism is positively recommended, the means of its attainment is one which obviously ought to be discussed and examined. Nothing could be more disastrous for Africa than that a false general attempt should be made. Already in Africa genuine regional unity is emerging, in the Ghana-Guinea-Mali Union, and in the foreshadowing of the East African Federation. These are species of unity which include a unanimity, or approximations thereto, in internal and international postures. It is this kind of genuine unity, rather than an after-dinner jollity and comradeship, which will save Africa. It is said that it took the United States a hundred and seventy years to achieve unity. At the same time, however, the pressures, both internal and external, bearing upon Africa are greater than those which the United States was called upon at its leisure to ameliorate. And Africa has proved that speed of action is one of its blessings. The dangers threatening a fragmented Africa, the impotence of schismatism, and the salvation of unity

are startlingly clear, much clearer than they could have been in
the early days of the United States. The history of the continents
is like the unfolding of Nebuchadnezzar's dream of the giant
whose sections were composed of different substances of growing scintillation. Africa, as pan-Africa, will prove to herself and
others that she has not got feet of clay. United, her future history
will be a history of splendour, scintillating with achievement
and variety, in unity and dignity.

INDEX